Printed and bound by CPI Group (UK) Ltd, Croydon, CR0 4YY

NBER

NATIONAL BUREAU *of* ECONOMIC RESEARCH

The Economics of Artificial Intelligence: Health Care Challenges

Edited by **Ajay Agrawal, Joshua Gans, Avi Goldfarb, and Catherine E. Tucker**

The University of Chicago Press

Chicago and London

The University of Chicago Press, Chicago 60637
The University of Chicago Press, Ltd., London
© 2024 by National Bureau of Economic Research
Published 2024
Printed in the United States of America

33 32 31 30 29 28 27 26 25 24   1 2 3 4 5

ISBN-13: 978-0-226-83311-8 (cloth)
ISBN-13: 978-0-226-83312-5 (e-book)
DOI: https://doi.org/10.7208/chicago/9780226833125.001.0001

Library of Congress Cataloging-in-Publication Data

Names: Agrawal, Ajay, editor. | Gans, Joshua, 1968- editor. | Goldfarb,
    Avi, editor. | Tucker, Catherine (Catherine Elizabeth), editor.
Title: The economics of artificial intelligence : health care challenges /
    edited by Ajay Agrawal, Joshua Gans, Avi Goldfarb, and Catherine
    E. Tucker.
Other titles: National Bureau of Economic Research conference report.
Description: Chicago : The University of Chicago Press, 2024. | Series:
    National Bureau of Economic Research conference report | Includes
    bibliographical references and index.
Identifiers: LCCN 2023037913 | ISBN 9780226833118 (cloth) | ISBN
    9780226833125 (ebook)
Subjects: LCSH: Medical economics. | Artificial intelligence—Medical
    applications.
Classification: LCC RA410.5 .E255 2024 | DDC 338.4/736210285—
    dc23/eng/20230921
LC record available at https://lccn.loc.gov/2023037913

♾ This paper meets the requirements of ANSI/NISO Z39.48-1992
(Permanence of Paper).

Relation of the Directors to the Work and Publications of the NBER

1. The object of the NBER is to ascertain and present to the economics profession, and to the public more generally, important economic facts and their interpretation in a scientific manner without policy recommendations. The Board of Directors is charged with the responsibility of ensuring that the work of the NBER is carried on in strict conformity with this object.

2. The President shall establish an internal review process to ensure that book manuscripts proposed for publication DO NOT contain policy recommendations. This shall apply both to the proceedings of conferences and to manuscripts by a single author or by one or more co-authors but shall not apply to authors of comments at NBER conferences who are not NBER affiliates.

3. No book manuscript reporting research shall be published by the NBER until the President has sent to each member of the Board a notice that a manuscript is recommended for publication and that in the President's opinion it is suitable for publication in accordance with the above principles of the NBER. Such notification will include a table of contents and an abstract or summary of the manuscript's content, a list of contributors if applicable, and a response form for use by Directors who desire a copy of the manuscript for review. Each manuscript shall contain a summary drawing attention to the nature and treatment of the problem studied and the main conclusions reached.

4. No volume shall be published until forty-five days have elapsed from the above notification of intention to publish it. During this period a copy shall be sent to any Director requesting it, and if any Director objects to publication on the grounds that the manuscript contains policy recommendations, the objection will be presented to the author(s) or editor(s). In case of dispute, all members of the Board shall be notified, and the President shall appoint an ad hoc committee of the Board to decide the matter; thirty days additional shall be granted for this purpose.

5. The President shall present annually to the Board a report describing the internal manuscript review process, any objections made by Directors before publication or by anyone after publication, any disputes about such matters, and how they were handled.

6. Publications of the NBER issued for informational purposes concerning the work of the Bureau, or issued to inform the public of the activities at the Bureau, including but not limited to the NBER Digest and Reporter, shall be consistent with the object stated in paragraph 1. They shall contain a specific disclaimer noting that they have not passed through the review procedures required in this resolution. The Executive Committee of the Board is charged with the review of all such publications from time to time.

7. NBER working papers and manuscripts distributed on the Bureau's web site are not deemed to be publications for the purpose of this resolution, but they shall be consistent with the object stated in paragraph 1. Working papers shall contain a specific disclaimer noting that they have not passed through the review procedures required in this resolution. The NBER's web site shall contain a similar disclaimer. The President shall establish an internal review process to ensure that the working papers and the web site do not contain policy recommendations, and shall report annually to the Board on this process and any concerns raised in connection with it.

8. Unless otherwise determined by the Board or exempted by the terms of paragraphs 6 and 7, a copy of this resolution shall be printed in each NBER publication as described in paragraph 2 above.

Contents

Acknowledgment

We gratefully acknowledge funding for this project from the Alfred P. Sloan Foundation.

Introduction

Ajay Agrawal, Joshua Gans, Avi Goldfarb,
and Catherine E. Tucker

Health care applications of artificial intelligence (AI) and machine learning (ML) have received a great deal of attention in academia. Over the past decade, a number of conferences have brought computer scientists and medical scholars together to develop AI health care tools. There are thousands of papers describing new ways to use AI in health care, and thousands more detailing what might go wrong as AI diffuses.

Despite this scholarly attention, AI adoption in health care has lagged other industries (Goldfarb, Taska, and Teodoridis 2020). To understand the potential for, and the barriers to, AI in health care, the second day of the 2022 National Bureau of Economic Research AI conference focused on AI, economics, and health care. Specifically, as set out in the invitation, "The goal of the day is to set the research agenda for economists, emphasizing how

Ajay Agrawal is the Geoffrey Taber Chair in Entrepreneurship and Innovation and professor of strategic management at the University of Toronto's Rotman School of Management, and a research associate of the National Bureau of Economic Research.

Joshua Gans is a professor of strategic management and holder of the Jeffrey S. Skoll Chair of Technical Innovation and Entrepreneurship at the Rotman School of Management, the University of Toronto, with a cross-appointment in the Department of Economics, and a research associate of the National Bureau of Economic Research.

Avi Goldfarb is the Rotman Chair in Artificial Intelligence and Healthcare and a professor of marketing at the Rotman School of Management, University of Toronto, and a research associate of the National Bureau of Economic Research.

Catherine E. Tucker is the Sloan Distinguished Professor of Management Science and professor of marketing at MIT Sloan, and a research associate of the National Bureau of Economic Research.

For acknowledgments, sources of research support, and disclosure of the authors' material financial relationships, if any, please see https://www.nber.org/books-and-chapters/economics-artificial-intelligence-health-care-challenges/introduction-economics-artificial-intelligence-health-care-challenges.

AI might enable a reimagining of the healthcare system and the economics of healthcare delivery."

Leading health economists were asked to write up and present ideas. Each presentation had two discussants, typically one with expertise in health care and one with expertise in machine learning. Other scholars attended from economics, machine learning, medicine, law, and public health, along with industry experts and clinicians.

This volume contains the four invited articles, along with commentary by a number of other attendees. As such it includes a multidisciplinary commentary rooted in the perspective of the health economists who wrote the articles. The papers and comments highlight the most important open questions for economists to address. Three themes emerge. First, each paper recognizes that AI has potential to improve health care, whether measured by better clinical outcomes or by reduced costs. Second, the papers identify different barriers to the successful deployment of AI in health care that may explain the current slow rate of adoption. Third, each paper offers at least a glimmer of hope for overcoming these barriers.

In terms of potential, Dranove and Garthwaite (chapter 1) note that advances in AI "offer new and unprecedented opportunities to improve medical decision-making." Sahni, Stein, Zemmel, and Cutler (chapter 2) estimate that AI could reduce health care costs by 5–10 percent, yielding hundreds of billions of dollars of savings in the United States each year. Mullainathan and Obermeyer (chapter 3) describe how AI can improve clinical outcomes, emphasizing an example of using AI to test for heart attack in the emergency department. Stern (chapter 4) cites the potential of contemporary deep learning to transform health care.

After recognizing this potential, the invited articles in this volume focus more on the barriers to successful adoption of AI. Each paper emphasizes a different headwind to AI's diffusion in health care: incentives (Dranove and Garthwaite), management (Sahni, Stein, Zemmel, and Cutler), data (Mullainathan and Obermeyer), and regulation (Stern).

Dranove and Garthwaite highlight the central role of the physician in the health care system. Therefore "the success of AI may depend on buy-in from the very individuals whose success it threatens—physicians." This threat to physicians comes from the potential for AI in diagnosis. Automated diagnosis "could result in physicians ceding much of their practices to lower-cost allied medical professionals." Given the central role of physicians in decision making, this represents an important barrier to adoption. If "development and adoption of AI for medical decision making will require the active participation of physicians and other medical decision makers before it is adopted," then broader changes to medical systems are needed, including in payment structures, decision rights, and malpractice risks. An AI that simply replaces physician diagnosis with machine diagnosis will face strong resistance from physician decision makers. Broadly, they emphasize the incentives of medical providers.

Bell, an executive at pharmaceutical company Novartis and former pharmacy professor, also emphasizes the central role of humans in the loop of medical decision making. Her emphasis is on the physician, and the recognition of the consequences of physician errors. AI has potential to reduce these errors and improve patient outcomes. She concludes, "We don't need to concern ourselves with replacing physicians just yet; let's just work on getting them all to play at the top of their game."

Sahni, Stein, Zemmel, and Cutler emphasize that "management barriers, both at the organizational level and industry level, have been the challenge in healthcare." They provide several specific examples of AI use cases, and argue against the barrier being related to physician payment schemes. Much of the paper is dedicated to measuring the potential impact of AI on health costs if these management barriers could be overcome, emphasizing not just improved clinical outcomes but also how AI could improve administrative efficiency.

Chan's comment on Sahni et al. seeks to understand these barriers by asking, "What makes technology adoption different in healthcare relative to other industries?" He notes that information technology (IT) adoption in health care was slow, and that a rich, data-driven literature developed to understand how economic incentives affected health IT. He concludes by asking for analysis that leverages heterogeneity in adoption of AI in health care, arguing that a closer look at "the effects of adoption on spending and outcomes would likely yield significant insights into the intended and unintended consequences of AI on the healthcare industry as a whole."

Sendak, Gulamali, and Balu discuss their experience developing and implementing over 15 AI solutions within Duke Health and their interviews of leaders across US health systems. The comment discusses the barriers to AI use in each of the delivery domains for patient care highlighted in Sahni et al. After specifying examples of AI implementation that address each of these domains, Sendak, Gulamali, and Balu highlight that "most health system and provider practice AI use cases do not generate financial value," especially under a fee-for-service reimbursement model. They highlight the need for several policy and organizational changes if AI solutions are going to be effective at scale.

Mullainathan and Obermeyer focus on "the lack of accessible clinical data." They describe the various barriers researchers and practitioners face in getting access to health data for building AI tools. First, identifying the necessary data requires deep knowledge of medicine, applied econometrics, and software engineering. Second, data access typically requires that the researcher have an appointment at a given hospital. They note that "even faculty members at universities affiliated with the hospital are typically ineligible." Any analyst working with the data is likely to need an appointment in the hospital, limiting the ability of academic researchers and AI companies to build clinical AI tools. They note that open data are a classic public good. "No single actor has a strong incentive to act." The paper argues that research is fundamental to the advancement of scientific fields, and that the challenges of accessing data for research mean that progress for AI in health care is slow.

Stern brings novel data on the regulation of medical AI to describe the ways in which the state of regulation has limited adoption of AI and other medical technologies. The barrier is not regulation per se. She notes that effective regulation can encourage adoption. Instead, the regulatory barriers relate to an uncertain regulatory environment and the challenges that software poses for medical regulation because of frequent updates. She emphasizes, "The value of regulatory innovation and regulatory clarity may be particularly important in the context of AI devices because such a large share of innovations to date have emerged from smaller firms and those from other countries" who may lack US regulatory expertise.

Each paper then offers some hope for overcoming these barriers. Dranove and Garthwaite emphasize the incentives within the medical system, particularly as they relate to the role of the physician. The last two sentences of the chapter provide a hint of how the barriers might be overcome: "A particularly important point is for actors from outside of healthcare to understand how the incentives of existing medical providers can influence the future of AI. This could highlight areas where a greater degree of intervention from outside of the sector may be warranted." In other words, changes in incentives that come from outside health care represent a way for health care to eventually benefit from AI's promise.

For Sahni, Stein, Zemmel, and Cutler, the hope comes through case studies, randomized control trials, and improved data that could be developed to prove the impact of AI in clinical domains. They note long timelines but that the overall promise of the technology suggests that the payoff may be worth the investment. Implicitly, they argue that demonstrated clinical and operational value can overcome incentive-related barriers.

After Mullainathan and Obermeyer's discussion of the data barriers, they describe steps they have taken to overcome these barriers. They are building two organizations, one nonprofit and one for-profit, to make data available to clinical researchers and practitioners. Their nonprofit, Nightingale Open Science, aims to catalyze research by supporting the creation of previously unseen datasets and making them accessible to a global community of researchers in ways that preserve patient privacy. Their for-profit, Dandelion Health, focuses on AI product development by building "the largest and highest-quality AI-ready training dataset in the world." This is perhaps an unusual role for academic economists. After recognizing that "it is perhaps surprising that market forces have not solved the problem of data access," they are trying to provide their own solutions.

Three comments focus on the access of these two organizations, and how to increase the chance that the data make a meaningful difference to health care globally. Eloundou and Mishkin, both of OpenAI, call for more data and discuss their organization's approach to developing models, which requires high-quality data and deep expertise in the model training phase.

Gichoya, a radiologist and informatician, emphasizes incentives for data sharing and legal and reputational risks as limiting the sharing of health care data. She highlights several of the competencies that Nightingale and Dandelion help deliver, concluding that they help with organization-level barriers related to "compliance, data science, finances, intellectual property, and legal expertise of data use agreements."

The comment by Papyan, Donoho, and Donoho (a mathematician-computer scientist, pediatric neurosurgeon, and statistician) provides a detailed discussion of the role of data platforms and how Mullainathan and Obermeyer's Nightingale initiative could lead "to the unleashing of a great deal of research energy as traditional barriers to research are shattered." They provide evidence that "the data platform concept—join researchers with data—has been proven to work in field after field across decades." Citing DARPA, IMAGENET, and MNIST, they make the bold claim that "from this viewpoint, [Turing Award winner] Yann LeCun made a bigger impact by developing the MNIST dataset and publishing it than by the specifics of any actual ML models he constructed for use with MNIST. Those early neural net models have been superseded, but MNIST is still powering research papers today." They also note that the success of data platforms typically hinges on rewards, and so economists should not ignore our expertise in incentives in developing and promoting health data platforms. The specific nature of such rewards and the data available through the platform should recognize advances in AI technology, recognizing that the goal is to incentivize the next generation of health care AI, the supply of data, and the development of models. They summarize, "By incorporating elements of the successful Common Task Framework, such as rewards and leaderboards, Nightingale can encourage participation and drive progress in the field."

Stern notes that many of the regulatory barriers are already being overcome. She notes "a dramatic uptick in the commercialization of AI products over recent years" and that "regulators have begun a germane and important discussion of how such devices could be regulated constructively in the future. Risk classification and the regulation of software updates are important areas for regulatory innovation. Compared to the other chapters, Stern's is relatively optimistic due to ongoing regulatory innovation. The right kind of regulation creates incentives to invest in new technology.

Babic, a philosophy professor, highlights Stern's data and analysis, noting that the increase in approvals of AI devices and the preliminary evidence on safety is encouraging. He provides some more detail on the regulatory innovation, building on Stern's chapter and Babic et al. (2019) to note that "the FDA [Food and Drug Administration] has required software-based medical devices to undergo a new round of review every time the underlying code is changed," and a new proposed framework, still in its infancy, "could make for a much more productive partnership between the FDA and medical AI manufacturers." He concludes that an alternative regulatory approach, with a separate agency for governing algorithms across all domains, would allow for a more AI-focused regulatory environment.

Several commenters touch on themes that appear in multiple papers. These comments mainly focused on strategies for overcoming the various barriers.

Operations professor Lu uses Sahni et al. to highlight the potential and then suggests ways that the physician resistance emphasized by Dranove and Garthwaite might be overcome. Specifically, with respect to physician resistance, she argues that "allowing physicians to freely choose whether to seek opinions from AI would greatly decrease the tension between physicians and AI and promote physician trust in AI."

Legal scholar Price recognizes "the key role of humans in the loop" while worrying that "not all healthcare providers will be able, adequately trained, or well resourced enough to catch errors in the system or to ensure it works as intended." He highlights how the anticipated use and the anticipated user affect design and regulation. The specific person in the loop matters. He notes that if "the value of AI systems in healthcare settings may in fact be greatest in situations where human experts are least available," then systems designed for an expert in the loop will eliminate much of the value of AI in health care.

Economists Bundorf and Polyakova also explore the changing role of the physician, building on ideas on Dranove and Garthwaite's chapter and using a framework familiar to economists: decision making under uncertainty. AI generates predictions, but clinical decision making is still likely to benefit from incorporating patient preferences. Patients may not have well-formed preferences over treatment outcomes, and so physicians and other medical professionals play a role in helping patients formulate preferences. Bundorf and Polyakova note that AI remains limited in its ability to predict such preferences and is likely to assume preference heterogeneity across patients. This, in turn, suggests a heterogeneous impact on clinicians. Those who are skilled at helping "patients translate prediction into decisions by incorporating patient preferences will have skills that are complementary to AI." Others will not. Ultimately, they note that an important aspect of the opportunity for AI to improve health care is to "incentivize physicians to focus on what medical students often say motivated them to choose medicine: listening to the patient."

Information systems professor Adjerid's comment discusses incentives and how technology can change the practice of health care. His insights come from research on the diffusion of electronic medical records, noting some parallels and a handful of differences. Epidemiologist Rosella also highlights lessons from electronic medical records, noting unintended negative consequences. Her comment discusses incentives, trust, and interface design.

We finish the volume with Rosella's conclusion as it effectively summarizes the four barriers highlighted in the papers, but reframes them as "the building blocks needed for AI to have a meaningful impact in healthcare": (1) designing AI to support the transparency needed in health care decisions (from Dranove and Garthwaite), (2) understanding of the complex health care environment (from Sahni et al.), (3) enriching the data used and ensuring it is made available in a responsible way (from Mullainathan and Obermeyer), and (4) creating innovative models of regulation (from Stern).

References

Babic, B., S. Gerke, T. Evgeniou, and I. Cohen. 2019. "Algorithms on Regulatory Lockdown in Medicine." *Science* 366 (6470): 1202–4.

Goldfarb, Avi, Bledi Taska, and Florenta Teodoridis. 2020. "Artificial Intelligence in Health Care? Evidence from Online Job Postings." *American Economic Association Papers & Proceedings* 110: 400–404.

Artificial Intelligence, the Evolution of the Health Care Value Chain, and the Future of the Physician

David Dranove and Craig Garthwaite

1.1 Introduction

It is often said that the most expensive medical "technology" is the physician's pen.[1] While this is an obviously apocryphal statement, it is rooted in the fundamental centrality of physicians to the health care economy. In his foundational book, Fuchs (1974) characterized the physician as the "captain of the team," i.e., the economic actor that directs the application of medical technology and as a result serves as the primary determinant of medical spending. Not much has changed in the fifty years since Fuchs advanced this argument—physicians still dominate medical decision making—except the team has gotten larger and much more expensive.

As the "captain of the team," physicians diagnose illnesses, recommend, and perform treatments. As described by Arrow (1963), patients trust their physicians to make the correct choices about their treatments and physicians continue to earn high scores in trust, especially when compared with other occupations (Gallup 2022). Yet physicians are fallible, often misdiagnosing

David Dranove is the Walter McNerney Distinguished Professor of Health Industry Management at Northwestern University's Kellogg School of Management, where he is also professor of strategy.

Craig Garthwaite is the Herman R. Smith Research Professor in Hospital and Health Services, a professor of strategy, and the director of the Program on Healthcare at Kellogg (HCAK) at Kellogg School of Management, Northwestern University, and a research associate of the National Bureau of Economic Research.

We thank Bingxiao Wu for her assistance in assembling tables 1.1 and 1.2. For acknowledgments, sources of research support, and disclosure of the authors' material financial relationships, if any, please see https://www.nber.org/books-and-chapters/economics-artificial-intelligence-health-care-challenges/artificial-intelligence-evolution-healthcare-value-chain-and-future-physician

1. See https://www.hcinnovationgroup.com/home/blog/13018116/whats-the-most-expensive-technology-the-doctors-pen.

cases and making the wrong treatment recommendations. Recent research has demonstrated that this can involve both undertreating those who are quite ill and overtreating those who are largely healthy (Mullainathan and Obermeyer 2021). The result is the undesirable combination of higher costs and increased rates of preventable death, injury, and illness.

Given the inherent fallibility of physicians, over the past several decades the medical community, payers, and regulators have experimented with incentive and provided physicians with information about best practices in an attempt to influence and improve medical decision making. A large research literature suggests that these efforts have had, at best, mixed results.[2]

Advances in data collection and analytic methods enabling the development of artificial intelligence (AI) offer new and unprecedented opportunities to improve medical decision making. Across a variety of cases, AI has shown the potential to reduce false positive and false negative rates of diagnosis. AI can also provide more appropriate treatment recommendations, often tailoring them to highly specific sets of symptoms and patient characteristics that could be difficult for every human medical provider to accurately diagnose. Finally, AI has the potential to overcome some inherent biases of various actors in the system, although this may be a matter of replacing the biases of physicians with the biases of data analysts and those who direct their work (Obermeyer et al. 2019).

To better understand the potential implications of AI in health care, we rely on the economic intuition established by Autor, Levy, and Murnane (2003), which examines the effect of greater automation on the distribution of wages and tasks across workers of different skill types. While Autor, Levy, and Murnane primarily consider the impact of robots doing relatively routine work, technological progress in AI means automation can increasingly accomplish some of the nonroutine tasks that were thought to be the solely the domain of human workers. They may even be able to accomplish some of these nonroutine tasks *better* than humans can.

But it is also apparent that other tasks routinely performed by physicians and other medical personnel remain well beyond the reach of even the most optimistic proponents of AI. As suggested by Autor (2022), the impact of a greater use of AI in medicine will therefore depend on the degree to which the routine and nonroutine tasks AI takes on complement or substitute for tasks that must still be performed by medical providers. As we discuss below, this impact will likely differ by specialty, skill set, and the patient's medical condition—with potentially wide-ranging ramifications for the medical profession.

Broadly speaking, physicians are responsible for both gathering information from patients and using that information to diagnose conditions

---

2. For example, see Wickizer and Lessler (2002) and Eijkenaar et al. (2013), which review the literature on utilization review and pay for performance, respectively.

and develop treatment protocols. To the extent the information gathered is purely physical (e.g., a blood sample, image, or tissue sample) and the diagnosis can be automated, physicians could conceivably lose their centrality in the role of "captain" and be replaced by medical providers serving as technicians carrying out the decisions made by third-party AI algorithms. This could result in physicians ceding much of their practices to lower-cost allied medical professionals, such as nurse practitioners working in retail clinics. In that case, value may be captured by the owners and implementors of the AI systems or the clinics or patients.

To the extent the information must still be gathered by interactions between human medical providers and patients, the ability to more accurately use that information to make a diagnosis and develop a treatment plan is a complement to a provider's effort. Providers who are better able to gather data from patients or utilize the additional information from AI may capture much of the valued created. However, that provider may not be the same type of doctor that currently completes those tasks—allied medical personnel may be equally (or more) capable of incorporating AI information into medical decisions. Therefore, AI's impact will be dictated by the set of tasks that currently comprise a physician's role in the system—which we demonstrate below varies meaningfully across specialties.

In the economic literature, the creation and adoption of AI is often either explicitly or implicitly modeled as an exogenous event emerging as a result of broader technological progress. In health care, however, there are a number of barriers to the success of AI that are specific to the sector and will likely influence the eventual existence and nature of automation. At a minimum, there are both institutional and legal barriers to assembling large data sets containing information about patients. Perhaps more importantly, the success of AI may depend on buy-in from the very individuals whose success it threatens—physicians. Accordingly, we discuss below how the predictions of ALM on the impact of AI on physicians are likely to also shape the types of AI that emerge and are adopted by the medical community.

In addition, we consider the role of government and the competitive environment in determining which types of technologies emerge. Absent some sort of standard-setting body, it is unclear how technologies will be adopted. This is particularly true if small differences emerge in the accuracy of these technologies and if the legal environment for liability is unclear.

We begin by describing important features of the health care market that are central to understanding the economic implications of AI. These include both the medical decision-making process and the history of third-party interventions. We next examine the implications of the labor economics literature on the distribution of economic surplus in the health care value chain and demonstrate the important role of different tasks in understanding this prediction. We conjecture about how AI will shape the future of physicians and allied personnel. We then take the perspective of AI firms—will they capture the value they create, and will they be forced to adapt to the potential backlash from physicians? We close with a discussion of additional areas of economic research that would help to understand the potential implications of AI in this market.

1.2   The Value Chain and Medical Decision Making

We begin by describing a highly stylized value chain in medical care, which highlights the central role of the physician. While the total value chain is quite complex, and includes medical innovation as well as health insurance, we focus on key steps from onset of illness to delivery of treatment:

- A patient visits a medical provider, usually a physician, either complaining of symptoms or for a routine check-up.
- The provider and the patient discuss the patient's health, and the provider performs additional diagnostic tests and procedures based on the information gleaned from the patient.
- The provider diagnoses any existing medical problems.
- The provider recommends a course of treatment, which may include watchful waiting, medication, additional diagnostic tests, and/or a surgical procedure.
- If the patient agrees, additional tests and treatment are rendered.

In a seminal paper, Arrow (1963) describes how and why physicians have played a central role in this health care value chain. Acting as learned agents for their patients, physicians help patients determine what medical services they require and who should provide them. Patients trust their physicians to be competent and compassionate. Physicians earn this trust through professional training as well as years of experience. Indoctrination during medical school as well as professional peer pressure further encourage physicians to serve as perfect, or near perfect agents (Dranove 1988). As Arrow put it, "The social obligation for best practice is part of the commodity that the physician sells."

Playing a central role in the value chain, physicians capture a sizable portion of the value they create. Physicians are among the highest-compensated individuals in the United States. For example, in 2017 the average physician earned nearly $350,000 per year, and half of all physicians were in the top two percent of all US earners (Gottlieb et al. 2020). These averages mask meaningful heterogeneity, with primary care physicians having an average income of approximately $250,000 and the average surgeon earning nearly $500,000. Allied medical providers, while still earning salaries that are well above average, do not approach these levels.

Other actors in the value chain, such as hospitals, drug and device makers, and even insurers, also contribute to value creation and capture an economically significant portion of that value as wages and profits. Patients capture the residual value—the difference between the health benefits created by the value chain and their payments in the form of both out-of-pocket spending and insurance premiums.

Almost as quickly as Arrow had described the physician–patient relationship, researchers began identifying ways in which the physician was far from a perfect agent. We discuss this research in the next section. Concerns about biases and errors have led both providers and third-party payers to use research evidence and practical experience to improve medical decision making. In the next section, we describe the history of these interventions with an underlying conceptual framework that AI is the latest and potentially most powerful example of these long-running efforts.

1.3   Third-Party Intervention in the Value Chain

Even before Arrow (1963) described the trustworthy physician-agent and Fuchs (1974) named physicians the "captain of the team," researchers were concerned about medical decision making. One line of research focused on the pernicious effects of fee-for-service reimbursements, which provided incentives to physicians to overtreat their patients.[3] The past fifty years have seen numerous efforts to remedy these potentially negative incentives.[4]

A second line of research on physician agency identified widespread variation in medical practice from doctor to doctor and across regions, such that seemingly identical patients often receive different treatments (Wennberg and Gittelsohn 1973; Cutler et al. 2019). To some extent, this could reflect differences in patient preferences or physician skills and might not indicate inefficiency (Chandra and Staiger 2007; Finkelstein, Gentzkow, and Williams 2016). There is a broad consensus, however, that at least some portion of practice variations reflects poor medical decision making, whether due to poor training, limited experience, or personal biases (Cutler et al. 2019). While most of the literature on inducement and practice variations focuses on their impact on health spending, a prominent 2000 report from the Institutes of Medicine provides alarming evidence of problems with quality that also reflected poor medical decision making (Kohn, Corrigan, and Donaldson 2000). Substandard quality may lead to over 100,000 unnecessary deaths annually in the United States.

If physicians are making poor decisions, it stands to reason that some oversight may be warranted.[5] There is a long history of medical providers

3. For example, see Shain and Roemer (1959), Roemer (1961), Evans (1974), Fuchs (1978), and Luft (1978).

4. These include the introduction of fixed payments per hospital admission (the DRG system), as well as a variety of payment innovations for physicians, often referred to as "payment reform." The latter may include bonuses based on following treatment guidelines or achieving quality metrics.

5. Much of this historical perspective is from Gray and Field (1989).

reviewing each other's decisions. For example, hospital quality assurance committees review medical records to assess the decisions of their medical staff. The first examples of third parties intervening in medical decision making date to the 1950s, when organizations including labor unions and some health maintenance organizations instituted second surgical opinion programs. As the name suggests, payers would not authorize reimbursement for a surgery without approval from an independent surgeon. Organized medicine resisted, and second opinion programs did not rapidly spread.

The Social Security Amendments of 1972 (PL 92-603) catalyzed third-party review by creating professional standards review organizations (PSROs). PRSOs were panels of local physicians that used their own expertise to develop "objective" standards of care for physicians practicing in their communities. By the late 1970s, a congressional subcommittee claimed that there were over two million unnecessary surgeries each year (American College of Surgeons, 1982). Congress authorized Medicare to augment PSROs with second surgical opinion programs, also developed by panels of independent physicians.

These programs worked via two distinct mechanisms that are salient to any consideration of modern AI. First, the review panels published their standards, which practicing physicians could use to inform their medical decisions. In this way, the panels would have complemented physician decision making. Second, the panels could review claims data and punish providers who failed to conform to the standards. In effect, physicians would have to follow the panel's recommendation or face punishment. In this way, the judgments of the panels would have substituted for physician decision making. As it turned out, the panels' guidelines were not well publicized, and the panels lacked meaningful punishment powers. As a result, the programs neither complemented nor substituted for physician decision making. In 1982, Congress replaced PSROs with peer review organizations (PROs), which had slightly stronger enforcement powers. Punishment remained relatively rare, however, and PROs were nearly as ineffective as PSROs.

While government oversight of medical decision making floundered, the private sector took notice of the potential benefits of these efforts. With employers grousing about rising health care benefits costs, commercial insurers introduced utilization review (UR) programs, essentially PROs with more meaningful teeth to match their bark. Insurers typically outsourced UR to independent companies. Interqual, one of the largest of these UR service providers, offers a good example of how UR worked.[6] Interqual would not authorize payment unless a case met two criteria. Intensity of service criteria included "diagnostic and therapeutic services generally requiring hospitalization," whereas severity of illness criteria included "objective,

6. This example drawn from Dranove (1993).

clinical parameters reflecting the need for hospitalization" (Interqual 1989). Interqual's medical advisors developed these criteria from literature reviews and their own experiences. Interqual developed computer algorithms to implement them. An Interqual employee (typically a nurse) could enter relevant clinical data and the algorithm would determine if the patient met the criteria. At the physician end of the interaction, a doctor would typically assign staff (again, typically a nurse) to provide the required data to Interqual. If the patient did not meet one or both of the criteria, the physician might get personally involved, providing further justification for the treatment decision.

Commercial UR programs intervened far more often than did PRSOs and PROs, and this led to a backlash from patients and physicians. Sixty percent of respondents to a 1998 Commonwealth Fund physician survey reported that they had serious problems with external reviews and limitations on their clinical decisions.[7] Physicians expressed concern about the impact on their patients' health. One common complaint was about the opacity of the UR algorithm. Another was that the physician possessed information about the patient that was not incorporated into the UR algorithm. How did the patient sound when they described their condition? How did the patient respond to prior treatments? Do they adhere to prescriptions? Do they have a supportive home environment?

Simply put, UR algorithms might produce the optimal treatment for a patient presenting with a limited, identifiable set of demographic and clinical characteristics. That is, UR can generate "norms" of care. But physicians have additional information about their patients' "idiosyncrasies" that the algorithm omits—often because there is not a plausible way for a physician to communicate the wealth of information that they have about each patient. This creates a tension: Is it better to force potentially biased physicians to conform to norms, or allow them to make their own decisions, factoring in idiosyncrasies? As we discuss, AI does not eliminate this tension, but it may tilt the calculus. This is particularly true if it becomes easier for AI systems to take in larger amounts of complex data.

What often grated on physicians about UR, and may apply equally well to AI, was that reviews were time consuming and cut into their incomes (at least as a measure of dollars per hour worked). A more subtle but potentially far more important factor was that UR threatened the physician's status as "captain of the team." If a computer algorithm could supplant the physician's judgment, this would totally subvert the value chain. Patients would no longer have to place their trust solely in the judgement of their

---

7. See "The Commonwealth Fund Survey of Physician Experiences with Managed Care," March 1997, https://www.commonwealthfund.org/publications/fund-reports/1997/mar/commonwealth-fund-survey-physician-experiences-managed-care.

physicians—they could, after all, get superior advice from a computer. This, in turn, could transform physicians from professionals whose judgments saved lives to technicians who merely followed directions, and could put the future earnings potential of physicians in jeopardy.

Politicians took notice of the backlash against UR. US House Minority Leader Steve Ellmann (R-MO) stated that "doctors and consumers . . . all have a horror story to tell you about the insurance company that wouldn't pay on the claim" (Hilzenrath 1997). Amid lobbying from organized medicine, many states enacted laws exposing insurers to malpractice regulations; we discuss below how these laws may impact AI. The US House of Representatives passed legislation that would prohibit insurers from overruling physician decisions, and President Clinton proposed a "Patient Bill of Rights" that would have provided recourse for patients when UR agencies denied coverage. Organized medicine widely praised these efforts.[8] Under intense political pressure, and with research studies failing to find consistent cost savings from UR, insurers changed course (Wickizer, Wheeler, and Feldstein 1989; Wickizer 1990). By the early 2000s, they no longer threatened to withhold payments from providers who failed to follow guidelines. Instead, UR would be purely informative.

For the next decade or longer, both the government and private insurers drew on an ever-growing volume of published research, as well as in-house data, to refine treatment guidelines. These remain almost exclusively informative rather than punitive. In the 2000s, the federal Agency for Healthcare Research and Quality sponsored nearly two dozen patient outcome research teams (PORTS), which developed treatment standards for a range of medical conditions, from lumbar spine stenosis and osteoarthritis to prostate cancer and heart attacks.[9] The PORTS developed standards by conducting meta-analyses of the relevant research literatures. Their recommendations came to be described as "evidence-based medicine" or "treatment protocols." When implemented by third parties such as health insurers or, increasingly, electronic health records (EHR) suppliers, these protocols are often referred to as clinical decision support (CDS).

As research evidence has grown, analysts have access to more granular EHR data. This means that the algorithms can incorporate information about what used to be "idiosyncrasies," more finely tailoring recommendations to specific patient needs. This tilts the calculus in favor of third-party oversight, and the evidence-based medicine movement has accelerated. Hospitals and/or payers often provide physicians with highly detailed

8. Reacting favorably to Clinton's proposal, American Medical Association president Thomas Reardon stated, "Restoring public confidence begins by allowing physicians to be advocates for their patients." Cited in "Clinton Proposes Patients' Bill of Rights," *British Medical Journal*, 1997, 315: 1397. For a discussion of the political jousting between organized medicine and health insurers, see Toner (2001).

9. For a detailed history of PORTS, see Freund et al (1999).

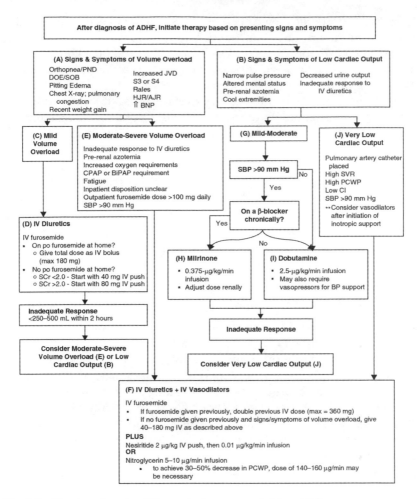

Fig. 1.1   Treatment protocol for acute decompensated heart failure

treatment protocols, indicating what tests to order, what diagnoses to render
based on test results, and what treatments to deliver based on diagnoses and
other pertinent patient information. Figure 1.1 depicts a treatment protocol for acute decompensated heart failure. Protocols are usually advisory,
and most physicians believe the positive aspects outweigh the negatives,
though a sizeable minority believe they limit their ability to make clinical

decisions.[10] For the most part, then, evidence-based medicine has served to complement existing physician practice.

AI represents the next step in the development of treatment protocols. By applying advanced data analytics to large data sets, computers incorporate ever more granular data and develop more sophisticated and fine-tuned protocols, including some that target very specific clinical indications. AI also offers new opportunities for oversight, not just of treatment recommendations, but of the diagnostic process. Up to now, a radiologist's reading of an MRI image or a pathologist's analysis of a tissue sample have been inputs into third-party algorithms. AI affords the opportunity to have machines read the MRIs and analyze the tissue samples. The potential for AI to either complement or substitute for physician practice is therefore spreading well beyond anything presented by prior third-party interventions. Understanding the implications for this widespread adoption of automation requires a clearer conceptual model of how such systems can impact the distribution of economic rents in the value chain.

1.4   Automation and the Distribution of Economic Value

Over the past several decades, technological progress has allowed for an increasing set of tasks to be completed by machines rather than humans. This began as primarily substituting for "blue collar" physical labor (e.g., steam shovels replacing physical shovels, tractors replacing horse-drawn plows) resulting in decreased employment among workers in those sectors (Rasmussen 1982; Olmstead and Rhode 2001). Eventually, advancements in computers allowed automation to move into more "white collar" professions resulting in declining employment for particular types of workers in those sectors (Autor 2014).

The ability of automation to undertake such tasks has caused a combination of consternation in the popular press and academic curiosity among researchers. These concerns focus on how the implementation of automation affects employment levels, wages, and inequality. Nonacademics have primarily focused on the ability of automation to substitute for workers and potentially decrease wages, often with doomsday predictions for the future of workers.

Economic theory, however, generates a far more ambiguous and heterogenous set of predictions about the impact of increased automation. Understanding the potential effects of automation requires starting from the idea that inputs to the value chain are generally rewarded based on their

10. Deloitte 2016 Survey of US Physicians, https://www2.deloitte.com/content/dam/Deloitte/us/Documents/life-sciences-health-care/us-lshc-physician-survey-hit-factsheet.pdf. Sixty-one percent of responding physicians agreed or strongly agreed with the statement "Overall, the positive aspects of having protocols outweigh the negatives." Forty-four percent agreed or strongly agreed that protocols "Limit physicians' ability to make clinical decisions."

productivity (Autor 2022). This productivity is itself a function of the input's capabilities (i.e., the economic value they can create) and its relative scarcity (i.e., the economic value it can potentially capture). Given the variety of ways in which value can be created and the changing nature of competition in the market, the productivity of inputs varies over time.

Predicting this variation in productivity requires considering that economic production is actually the result of a bundles of tasks, some of which are accomplished by labor and some by capital. The mix of these inputs varies meaningfully by occupation and over time, as the degree to which production can rely on labor and capital is a function of technological progress. While each of these tasks for production are necessary, changes in the relative cost of each type of input will vary the optimal mix of tasks and the optimal use of labor and capital. It will also be a function of the degree to which newly developed technologies create a *displacement effect* by simply replacing tasks done by labor or a *productivity effect* by increasing the value of other types of labor inputs. To the extent that these new capital inputs raise the value of labor, they will increase rather than decrease demand for these types of labor. Thus, labor may increase from automation, but the effect will vary across the distribution of workers (see Acemoglu and Restrepo 2020 for a discussion of these effects and a broader discussion of the labor economic research into the effects of automation).

Perhaps the most canonical study in this task-based approach of considering automation is Autor, Levy, and Murnane (2003). The authors focus on a task-based approach to the impacts of automation on wages and inequality and posit that to the degree economic value is created by a combination of tasks, the role of increased automation is a function of how it affects the relative contribution of these tasks to create economic value.

Autor, Levy, and Murnane break tasks up into two broad categories—routine and nonroutine. At the time the paper was written, technological limitations meant automation was primarily relegated to completing "routine" tasks, those that follow a well-defined set of rules and an order of operations that can be clearly documented and communicated to computers in the form of a program. These categories resulted from the limits of computer programming and technology at that time. Tacit human knowledge was difficult to communicate to computers, and this served as a fundamental boundary between the types of tasks that could be automated and those that could not. This, in turn, provided some clear bounds of the amount of substitution that could occur.

Autor, Levy, and Murnane illustrate how the impact of automation depends on the degree to which new technologies serve as a substitute or a complement for the work currently done by humans. They find that the rise of automation in routine tasks resulted in a reduction in labor inputs for those tasks. They also found that as the costs of automating routine tasks fell, there was an increase in demand for labor performing nonroutine tasks that were complements to automation. Over time, technology progressed so that even more routine tasks could be automated, with subsequent declines in clerical and administrative occupations (Autor 2014). This trend has continued with the rise of industrial robots, i.e., autonomous machines that can complete well defined tasks without human oversight. Acemoglu and Restrepo (2020) find that the increased use of industrial robots for tasks such as welding, painting, and manufacturing is responsible for a decline in employment for these sectors.

Some described the advent of AI, and its ability to accomplish tasks that cannot be specifically programmed, as overturning that paradigm discussed in Autor, Levy, and Murnane 2003 (e.g., Susskind 2020). In reality, advances in AI have simply shifted the frontier of jobs that could be automated from purely routine tasks to the nonroutine tasks that were reserved for humans identified by Autor, Levy, and Murnane. We posit that while this has clear implications for which types of tasks could ultimately be automated, the fundamental economic points remain largely unchanged and will continue to dictate the distribution of rents across the value chain. Ultimately, the impact of AI-based automation will be a function of the degree to which it displaces labor inputs or increases the productivity of other types of labor inputs—noting that even advancements that increase productivity could result in a net decline of economic rents collected by labor. We also note that the impact of AI could vary greatly across the distribution of workers as certain types of labor may find their tasks are less replaceable than others.

1.5   Modeling AI in Health Care

We draw on this labor economics literature to consider the variety of ways that an increased use of AI could impact the distribution of value in health care. As we consider the relative impact of AI on various actors in the value chain, there are questions both about the degree of complementarity and the relative scarcity of various types of employees. For example, consider a situation where the widespread adoption of AI for diagnostic testing allowed for more medical decision making to be completed by midlevel providers such as physician assistants or nurse practitioners rather than doctors. This would increase the value that could be created by these midlevel providers. However, there are relatively fewer restrictions on entry for this profession, and as a result new workers could be attracted into this sector. As a result, while the value created by the shift to midlevel providers could be quite high, it is not clear whether those providers would capture much of it.

As a starting point, we must consider the appropriate definition of "productivity" in this context. As discussed by Autor, Levy, and Murnane (2003), productivity is the result of the amount of value created and the scarcity of an input in creating the value. Inputs are rewarded based on their productivity. In our context of medical decision making, productivity is related to the inputs used to reach a medical decision and the quality of that medical decision. For example, imagine that the true diagnosis sits along a line or around a circle. There is some reported diagnosis, based on labor and AI inputs, that sits on the same line or circle. The smaller the distance between the reported and true diagnosis, the better the health outcome for the patient. (One can easily include costs into the calculus.) In this way, productivity can be equated to the proximity of the true and reported diagnosis. Likewise for the productivity of the treatment decision. Thus, there is a natural correspondence between productivity as defined by Autor, Levy, and Murnane and productivity in medicine.

Historically, productivity in medicine was primarily the result of a physician's effort with little reliance on technology or third parties. We have discussed how third parties use evidence-based medicine to improve productivity in treatment recommendations. While the jury is out regarding the magnitude of these improvements, there is little doubt that technological change has led to substantial improvements in diagnostic productivity—contrast MRIs with X-rays to diagnose breast cancer, for example. Some new diagnostics require very little judgement or insight. For example, a cholesterol test produces a specific number measuring heart health, and a blood test for measuring glomerular filtration rate provides a clear estimate of kidney function. In these settings, there is little expertise required to perform or interpret the test. Instead, physicians are primarily responsible for knowing which tests to order and what to recommend given a particular set of results. While that frontier of recommendations is obviously moving over time, it is not particularly cumbersome for physicians to follow the frontier in their specialty.

Other innovations, including imaging and genetic tests, require more physician input into reading and interpreting test results. For example, radiologists have historically been critical to reading scans to detect various cancers or other abnormalities. Similarly, orthopedic surgeons read images such as MRIs and X-rays to determine whether patients are candidates for surgeries as opposed to other more conservative interventions. Developing treatment plans from testing that requires more judgement currently requires patients and third-party payers to rely even more heavily on the recommendation of a medical provider.

Let us return to the notion that productivity reflects the difference between true and reported diagnosis/treatment recommendation. It is important to recognize that even if the physician knows what is best for the patient, with no uncertainty, the physician might not truthfully report what is best. Unlike other settings of increased use of automation, where the firm that employs AI will choose the most productive use, it may not be financially advantageous for the physician to use AI. More importantly, the physician might not be constrained by market forces to use it. Consider the case of patients with back pain. Some of these patients may require surgery to address their underlying condition—a treatment plan that may generate significant value for the provider. Of course, there are other patients with back pain that results from less severe underlying medical conditions that would benefit from a more conservative path such as physical therapy and weight management. In a world where the physician is independently responsible for developing and reporting a treatment plan, that physician may recommend surgery when it is unwarranted but financially beneficial to the physician. This may reflect both demand inducement and practice variations that we discussed earlier.

If AI serves the same function as PORTS or treatment protocols—informational but not dictatorial—then demand inducement and practice variations may still lead to suboptimal decisions. Even so, the introduction of AI may lead to far superior outcomes than existing treatment protocols, for several reasons. First, to the extent that AI provides more accurate diagnoses and treatment decisions than even the best current protocols, physicians will increasingly accept its recommendations. This may have a secondary benefit. In an effort to reduce medical spending, insurers have attempted to force physicians to take financial responsibility when their patients' costs exceed various benchmarks. Physicians often resist, arguing that medical costs are too unpredictable. AI can add predictability to both diagnoses and treatment costs, encouraging more physicians to accept payment reforms. Second, accurate AI would give insurers more confidence to challenge physician decisions. In effect, the insurer may prefer an unbiased decision based solely on AI input over a potentially biased physician-determined weighting of AI and physician input. Consider further that while most physicians have not embraced payment reform, many hospitals have, in the form of accountable care organizations and other new payment structures. AI may give hospitals the tools to accurately evaluate the productivity of their own medical staff. Physicians may prefer following treatment recommendations offered by their hospital employers more than from commercial insurers.

Another economically important feature of AI is the ability to use a different combination of inputs in the medical decision-making process. Suppose, for example, that there is some nontrivial fixed cost to physicians reading radiology scans or tissue samples. If AI reading of scans and tissue samples is sufficiently inexpensive and sufficiently accurate, it would be efficient to bypass the physician altogether. As some of our examples show, AI diagnostic accuracy can far exceed what physicians have accomplished, even when physicians incorporate AI into their diagnoses. We suspect that radiologists and pathologists have much to be concerned about as AI use expands into more areas of diagnosis. If industrial robots can replace welders, painters, and others in the broader economy, then can these medical specialists be far behind?

Can the same be said for broader areas of medical decision making? Can robots replace doctors? Rendering diagnoses and making treatment recommendations often require information from patients about their underlying health. Traditionally, physicians obtain this information during office visits and incorporate it into their "personal algorithms." Even if gathering of this information is a crucial step in the value chain, there may be no reason why the physician needs to be involved. This information could be gathered by a midlevel provider such as a physician assistant or a nurse practitioner. To the extent that the information and resulting decisions are colored by various nuances, such as the patient's affect when responding to questions, it might not be sufficient for a midlevel provider to feed the answers to rote questions into a computer. We lack the expertise to state which types of conditions have such subjectivity in reporting, but this seems likely to be an important determinant of when midlevel providers will effectively substitute for physicians. We also note that it is not immediately clear whether physicians are the optimal labor input even when information requires some subjectivity.

Questions about this type of substitution are particularly important because different medical providers take part in related but distinct labor markets. As we discuss below, both wages and entry into these labor markets can be sticky, leading to long run inefficiencies in the labor market response to AI.

1.5.1   Examples of a Task-Based Approach to Examining the Economic Effects of AI on the Health Care Value Chain

This discussion makes it obvious that the distribution of a physician's tasks and the availability of substitute inputs is a key factor in determining value capture. This set of tasks differs by specialty (and likely within specialty across geography and setting). Better understanding which specialties will be most impacted by AI requires examining this variation in the nature of tasks performed and how it intersects with existing and potential AI technology.

To provide a simple illustration of this variation, tables 1.1 and 1.2 list the most common procedures and services delivered to Medicare beneficiaries by two specialists—general internal medicine and radiologists.[11] Table 1.1 ranks the top ten procedures and services by frequency; table 1.2 ranks them by payments.

While nonmedical experts often refer to the profession of a "physician" fairly generically, these lists of job tasks demonstrate the fundamental heterogeneity across different specialties of physicians. Of particular interest is the extent to which the specialties differ in the extent of interaction with patients. As the tables and exhibit show, not surprisingly, radiologists primarily bill payers for their engagements with technology. Radiologists largely read X-ray, CT, MRI, and other diagnostic images; the actual imaging (and engagement with patients) is usually performed by allied medi-

---

11. We are grateful to Bingxiao Wu for assembling these data.

Table 1.1   Top 10 procedures and services in 2020 (ranked by total number of Medicare services)

Radiology

Rank	Service	Number of Medicare services (in millions)
1	X-ray scan	32
2	CT scan	18.9
3	Ultrasound examination	7.2
4	Mammography	6.1
5	MRI scan	5.1
6	Digital tomography	4.8
7	Bone density measurement	1.6
8	Nuclear medicine study	0.7
9	Imaging for evaluation of swallowing function	0.2
10	Biopsy	0.2

Internal Medicine

Rank	Service	Number of Medicare services (in millions)
1	Injection of drug	30.8
2	Established patient office or other outpatient service	27.9
3	Subsequent hospital inpatient care	18.9
4	Blood test	8.1
5	Insertion of needle into vein for collection of blood sample	5.4
6	Vaccine	5.4
7	Subsequent nursing facility visit	5.1
8	Annual wellness visit	3.7
9	Initial hospital inpatient care	3.5
10	Hospital discharge day management	3.0

Source: 2020 Medicare utilization and payment data, Physicians & Other Practitioners, at the provider-service level, https://data.cms.gov/provider-summary-by-type-of-service/medicare-physician-other-practitioners/medicare-physician-other-practitioners-by-provider-and-service.

cal personnel under the radiologist's supervision. In contrast, internists are primarily billing for their interactions with patients. The tables and exhibit show that these physicians earn most of their income directly engaging with patients, in office and hospital visits of varying length.

It is also important to note that these particular tasks represent what physicians are able to bill for but fall short of providing a comprehensive description of the tasks necessary to complete these activities. As a result, while a typology based solely on billing codes makes it seems that radiology is devoid of human contact and internists are neo-luddites who eschew technology, the reality is far more complex.

Table 1.2   **Top 10 procedures and services in 2020 (ranked by total Medicare payment)**

Radiology

Rank	Service	Medicare payment (in $ millions)
1	CT scan	1,130
2	MRI scan	526
3	Mammography	405
4	Ultrasound examination	322
5	X-ray scan	284
6	Nuclear medicine study	184
7	Digital tomography	176
8	Removal of plaque in arteries	149
9	Bone density measurement	32.3
10	Biopsy	29.9

Internal Medicine

Rank	Service/procedure	Medicare payment (in $ millions)
1	Established patient office or other outpatient service	1,760
2	Subsequent hospital inpatient care	1,300
3	Initial hospital inpatient care	511
4	Annual wellness visit	458
5	Subsequent nursing facility visit	328
6	Hospital discharge day management	237
7	Injection of drug	226
8	Vaccine	221
9	Critical care delivery	135
10	Physician telephone patient service	107

Ultimately, the services each type of physician bills involve a combination of tasks with varying degrees of technology and human interaction. To demonstrate the complexity of tasks that underlie the billing codes in tables 1.1 and 1.2, exhibit 1.1 contains the tasks that are identified by the Occupational Information Network (O*Net) to define the occupation of a radiologist and a general internal medicine physician. Examining these tasks makes it immediately clear that a billing-based classification of activities that implies radiologists only interact with technology and internists solely work with human patients is overly simplistic.

At a minimum, radiologists must report their findings to physicians. While reports to other physicians are usually written rather than verbal, they can often contain the kind of nuance that might be difficult for AI to fully repli-

Exhibit 1.1

O*Net Tasks for Radiologists

- Obtain patients' histories from electronic records, patient interviews, dictated reports, or by communicating with referring clinicians.
- Prepare comprehensive interpretive reports of findings.
- Perform or interpret the outcomes of diagnostic imaging procedures including magnetic resonance imaging (MRI), computer tomography (CT), positron emission tomography (PET), nuclear cardiology treadmill studies, mammography, or ultrasound.
- Review or transmit images and information using picture archiving or communications systems.
- Communicate examination results or diagnostic information to referring physicians, patients, or families.
- Provide counseling to radiologic patients to explain the processes, risks, benefits, or alternative treatments.
- Instruct radiologic staff in desired techniques, positions, or projections.
- Confer with medical professionals regarding image-based diagnoses.
- Coordinate radiological services with other medical activities.
- Document the performance, interpretation, or outcomes of all procedures performed.
- Establish or enforce standards for protection of patients or personnel.
- Develop or monitor procedures to ensure adequate quality control of images.
- Recognize or treat complications during and after procedures, including blood pressure problems, pain, oversedation, or bleeding.
- Participate in continuing education activities to maintain and develop expertise.
- Participate in quality improvement activities including discussions of areas where risk of error is high.
- Perform interventional procedures such as image-guided biopsy, percutaneous transluminal angioplasty, transhepatic biliary drainage, or nephrostomy catheter placement.
- Develop treatment plans for radiology patients.
- Administer radioisotopes to clinical patients or research subjects.

Exhibit 1.1 (cont.)

- Advise other physicians of the clinical indications, limitations, assessments, or risks of diagnostic and therapeutic applications of radioactive materials.
- Calculate, measure, or prepare radioisotope dosages.
- Check and approve the quality of diagnostic images before patients are discharged.
- Compare nuclear medicine procedures with other types of procedures, such as computed tomography, ultrasonography, nuclear magnetic resonance imaging, and angiography.
- Direct nuclear medicine technologists or technicians regarding desired dosages, techniques, positions, and projections.
- Establish and enforce radiation protection standards for patients and staff.
- Formulate plans and procedures for nuclear medicine departments.
- Monitor handling of radioactive materials to ensure that established procedures are followed.
- Prescribe radionuclides and dosages to be administered to individual patients.
- Review procedure requests and patients' medical histories to determine applicability of procedures and radioisotopes to be used.
- Teach nuclear medicine, diagnostic radiology, or other specialties at graduate educational level.
- Test dosage evaluation instruments and survey meters to ensure they are operating properly.

O*Net Tasks for General Internal Medicine Physicians

- Analyze records, reports, test results, or examination information to diagnose medical condition of patient.
- Treat internal disorders, such as hypertension, heart disease, diabetes, or problems of the lung, brain, kidney, or gastrointestinal tract.
- Prescribe or administer medication, therapy, and other specialized medical care to treat or prevent illness, disease, or injury.
- Manage and treat common health problems, such as infections, influenza, or pneumonia, as well as serious, chronic, and complex illnesses, in adolescents, adults, and the elderly.

(continued)

Exhibit 1.1 (cont.)

- Provide and manage long-term, comprehensive medical care, including diagnosis and nonsurgical treatment of diseases, for adult patients in an office or hospital.
- Explain procedures and discuss test results or prescribed treatments with patients.
- Advise patients and community members concerning diet, activity, hygiene, and disease prevention.
- Make diagnoses when different illnesses occur together or in situations where the diagnosis may be obscure.
- Refer patient to medical specialist or other practitioner when necessary.
- Monitor patients' conditions and progress and reevaluate treatments as necessary.
- Collect, record, and maintain patient information, such as medical history, reports, or examination results.
- Provide consulting services to other doctors caring for patients with special or difficult problems.
- Advise surgeon of a patient's risk status and recommend appropriate intervention to minimize risk.
- Immunize patients to protect them from preventable diseases.
- Direct and coordinate activities of nurses, students, assistants, specialists, therapists, and other medical staff.
- Prepare government or organizational reports on birth, death, and disease statistics, workforce evaluations, or the medical status of individuals.
- Conduct research to develop or test medications, treatments, or procedures to prevent or control disease or injury.
- Operate on patients to remove, repair, or improve functioning of diseased or injured body parts and systems.
- Plan, implement, or administer health programs in hospitals, businesses, or communities for prevention and treatment of injuries or illnesses.

---

cate. To the extent that radiology reports are formulaic (e.g., they characterize the size and nature of an observed lesion or cyst and state a probability that the lesion or cyst is malignant), AI might be able to produce the same type of report, with greater accuracy. However, there could still be tasks that are necessary for a radiologist to complete in partnership with these results. For example, radiologists also must often work with patients to help them to understand their testing procedures and results—a task that would be hard to imagine being supplanted by AI in the near future.

Nor do the findings from claims data mean that all tasks involved with being an internist require the types of patient interactions that cannot be overtaken by advances in AI. As exhibit 1.1 shows, internists need to be able to accurately diagnose medical conditions from a variety of data, order appropriate tests, and make treatment recommendations for patients. As the task list demonstrates, this is often based on information about a variety of symptoms and ailments, and advanced AI could do better at both diagnosing and identifying treatments in those cases. Even in that case, a medical provider is critical to gather information for the AI system. However, there is no definitive reason that task needs to be completed by a physician. Allied medical personnel can and often do engage in these kinds of patient interactions. To the extent those personnel can serve as a complement to advances in AI, the centrality of even physicians who currently interact a lot with patients could be threatened.

1.6   AI in Medical Practice

Fully understanding the potential scope for automation to serve as either a substitute or a complement for physician productivity requires more knowledge about the types of AI that have currently been developed or could conceivably emerge over a reasonable time frame.

Taking a step back, we note that while technological progress has allowed AI to take part in nearly all aspects of medical practice, at a broad level, these technologies fall into two primary categories:[12]

- *Scanning of test samples to perform diagnoses.* Radiologists visually assess medical images to detect and characterize disease (Hosny et al. 2018). AI algorithms are particularly effective in recognizing and interpreting complex images and therefore may produce faster and more accurate diagnoses than human physicians (Alkhaldi 2021). For example, Kim et al. (2020) partnered with five hospitals to collect mammography scans and patient outcome data. They found that AI improved the detection of breast cancer, with false negative rates falling from 25 percent to 15 percent. The greatest improvement was for early-stage cancers, which are hardest to detect. Mawatari et al. (2020) found that when radiologists relied on deep convolutional neural network (DCNN) software that was trained using data from one hospital to detect hip fractures, false negative rates fell from 17 percent to 9 percent.[13] AI can also aid in the screening of blood and tissue samples. For example, Hollon et al.

---

12. The lone exception, surgery, faces disruption from another new technology: robots.
13. When radiologists incorporated DCNN results but also considered their own independent reading of images, false negative rates increased to 12 percent.

(2020) studied the time required to interpret histologic images during cancer surgery performed on over 400 patients at one hospital. The surgeon must wait while the samples are read, so every minute counts. They found that DCNN reduces the time required for the pathologist to analyze samples from 40 minutes to 3 minutes, with no difference in accuracy.

- *Mining of clinical data*: Data mining—identifying reproduceable patterns in big data—has several potential uses in health care, from extracting relevant information from EHRs to forecasting diseases before they happen, to recommending treatments tailored to highly detailed clinical information. Mining EHRs can turn up health indicators that predict the onset of disease. For example, the US Department of Veterans Affairs, partnering with DeepMind Health, developed a model to predict acute kidney injury during hospital stays. The model incorporates new health data as it is entered into the EHR and predicts 90 percent of kidney injuries that would require dialysis up to 48 hours before the injury. Such early prediction allows doctors to take steps to reduce the progression of the injury and potentially prevent the need for dialysis. The model also indicates the relevant clinical factors that led to the prediction and the relevant blood tests for monitoring the patient.

Broadly these tasks fall under the category of CDS, which represents a potentially far-reaching use of data mining. An important task for physicians is to translate diagnostic information into treatment recommendations, from which drugs to prescribe to whether the patient requires major surgery. These decisions can be highly complex, involving dozens of clinical indicators (Croskerry 2018). AI can digest information in published research as well as mine thousands of clinical records to identify the best treatments to recommend, at a granularity that is limited only by the size of the data set and the range and precision of variables included in the data. In an early application, the University of North Carolina Cancer Center used IBM Watson's Genomic project to personalize treatments for patients with specific genetic defects (Patel et al. 2018). Admittedly, the use of Watson also stands as evidence of existing limitations with AI. However, it is unclear how binding this limitation will be over time.

These two categories of AI both contribute toward the ultimate goal of medical practice: obtaining an appropriate diagnosis and treatment plan that increases a patient's health. Of course, the economic implications of these two types of AI developments could be vastly different.

We also note that while these are the two broad areas that AI *could* fall into, there has been far more development of diagnostic tools that substitute for potential physician effort. The development of sophisticated CDS that truly guides physicians or other medical providers has not fully emerged into the market. This could, of course, be a function of simple technological progress. However, as we discuss in the next section, there are a variety of economic and market-based barriers that could limit the development of particular types of AI.

1.7   Barriers to AI Development and Implementation

To the degree that automation decreases the value captured by traditional medical providers, it will create opportunities for other parts of the value chain to capture value. As such, we also discuss below how the effect of AI on the value chain affects the market for developing new AI in this sector. The existing labor economics literature on the role of automation often thinks of these technological developments as exogenous—and often in the case of manufacturing or more generic routine tasks, this is a reasonable assumption. However, the development and adoption of AI for medical decision making will require the active participation of physicians and other medical decision makers before its adopted.

While AI has the potential to serve the two broad features of performing diagnoses and supporting clinical decision making, to date we have primarily seen it adopted in a role of diagnosis. Even in the role where AI is being developed to serve a diagnostic role, its widespread adoption has been more limited than some would have expected if one only considers the pace of technological progress.

Some of this lack of adoption both within and across categories could be the result of different applicability of technologies. However, we would argue that in addition to any pure technological features, there are a number of economic factors that have limited the adoption of these services.

1.7.1   Access to Data

Regardless of its application, AI requires data, from scans, blood samples, clinical and outcome data from medical records, and so on. These data largely reside in EHRs and, in principle, are already available for data scientists to explore (though we also are aware that some valuable data currently resides in the minds of physicians). In some countries, such as England, EHRs are universal, uniform, and consolidated—all data is centralized and uniformly reported. In the United States, however, data are fragmented across many EHR systems with limited interoperability. That is, data exchange across platforms is limited. Moreover, even when providers use the same platform, there is substantial customization, which again limits data exchange.

There are also regulatory barriers to assembling and using medical data. Data are protected by the Health Insurance Portability and Accountability Act of 1996 (HIPAA), which can limit the sharing of personally identifiable health information across medical providers. This makes it extremely difficult for third parties to access claims data and to pool data across providers or over time; Tschider (2019) calls this "the healthcare privacy–artificial intelligence impasse." This barrier is particularly problematic for the many technology-focused firms that are attempting to develop health care for AI but exist outside of the traditional medical system. Even if HIPAA were relaxed to allow for more data sharing, one could argue that the sensitive nature of the data increases fears of litigation or other negative events when working with such data from outside of your own firm.

The upshot is that in the United States, analytics are often confined to "in-house" data, often from a single hospital or health system. Indeed, the published literature on AI is replete with studies derived from surprisingly small samples drawn from individual hospitals and systems. An important exception are studies involving the US Veterans Administration, which bills itself as the largest integrated health care system in the country. With EHRs covering 9.1 million patients, the VA has proven to be fertile ground for AI development.[14] The VA has even established a National Artificial Intelligence Institute and has published numerous studies of AI in the VA system.[15] Kaiser Permanente, the largest private integrated health system, is also active in AI development. Kaiser and other large systems may find AI becoming a new source of value creation, as their privately developed diagnostic tools and CDS systems give them an edge over smaller providers lacking access to similar data.

As large health systems continue to facilitate AI development, it is unclear how the resulting decision tools will filter out into general use. Systems may want to protect their intellectual property so as to maintain competitive advantage. Even if systems feel charitable, sharing their algorithms may require compromises to accommodate variations in the kinds of data available in different EHRs. It is also concerning whether any relative homogeneity of the patients or the practice of medicine in these organizations could lead to biased AI technologies. This is particularly true when, as we describe below, part of the process of AI involves developing ways in which automation can occur through processes that are not immediately obvious or knowable by humans. Quite simply, as the machine learns, we may not be fully aware what it is learning and whether there is truly external validity to these processes.

Many health insurers have significant skills in data analytics. So too do many companies outside of health care. In order to access and use sensitive health data without running afoul of HIPAA, these companies may need to own the provider practices that generate the data. This may partially explain the integration strategy of Optum, which is the nation's leading employer of physicians. In the absence of widespread data sharing, the potential for both

14. See https://www.research.va.gov/naii/.
15. For example, see Piette et al. (2016), Lee et al. (2021), Rodriguez-Diaz et al. (2021), and Jing et al., (2022)

value creation and value capture by large vertically integrated organizations using in-house data to develop AI systems may be palpable.

1.7.2   Sticky Prices and Entry Barriers

AI will reduce the productivity gap between physicians and allied medical professionals for at least some medical services. In a well-functioning market, we would expect physician fees for the affected services to fall. In equilibrium, physicians might continue to provide these services, albeit at lower wages that reflect the reduced scarcity of their ability in these new production functions. In the long run, declining physician compensation would likely reduce entry by new physicians and drive up the fees for those services not affected by AI or those that are complements to AI and can only be performed by physicians.

The idiosyncrasies of physician fee schedules, however, suggest that this dynamic may not play out exactly as predicted by economic models from outside of health care. Medicare and most private insurers use the resource-based relative value scale (RBRVS) as the basis for setting a fee schedule. Even when private insurers pay a multiple of the Medicare rate, the *relative* value of these services is dictated by this schedule unless the payer engages in effort to separately negotiate the fee (Clemens, Gottlieb, and Molnár 2017).

The RBRVS assigns each of several thousand different physician services a relative value unit (RVU). The fee for any given service is the corresponding RVU for that service, multiplied by a dollar multiplier. The Centers for Medicare and Medicaid Services sets the multiplier for services delivered to Medicare beneficiaries. Private insurers either set or negotiate a separate multiplier for their enrollees. The important point is that the relative fees for all services are dictated by the RVU, and that RVUs are based on the resource inputs required to produce the service—essentially physician and office staff time and overhead. In other words, the relative fees for different services are effectively based on a labor theory of value rather than on the productivity of the input. Market forces only enter to the extent that they influence the overall multiplier and not the relative value of various tasks.[16]

The implication is that while AI may reduce the relative productivity of certain physician services, it is not likely to lead to a reduction in the relative fees for those services. To the extent that AI affects fees, it will depend on whether AI increases or decreases the amount of time it takes for physicians to render a final diagnosis/recommendation. It is not clear which direction this will go.

Sticky fees will accelerate the shift away from using physicians for ser-

---

16. Some payers set or negotiate separate fees for a small number of "carved-out" services, such as joint replacement surgery and deliveries of newborns. These fees may be based on market forces. The lion's share of reimbursements are based on RVUs.

vices where their productivity advantage has declined. After all, if a physician has become far less productive relative to affiliated medical providers but wages have not adjusted to reflect this decline, payers may be more inclined to use the affiliated provider. What is interesting, and is an area for more research, is the situation where the productivity advantage has declined but the best potential medical outcome is still the result of the combination of a physician with the newly developed AI technologies. In these settings, there could be a conflict between what is the most effective and what is the most cost-effective treatment—particularly if the wages of physicians are unable to adjust. It is a broader political economic question as to how such conflict would be resolved, but given the history of physician reimbursement and the role of policymakers on limiting the ability of payers to dictate care, it is not obvious that we would reach the most economically efficient outcome.

As the prices for various services evolve in a market, we would normally expect the entry and exit of affected economic actors. Various frictions in the form of entry and exit barriers would, however, limit this movement. This is particularly evident in the labor market for medical providers where a variety of credentialing organizations limit the free flow of individuals into the market. However, these barriers are not the same across different actors. For example, there are far more limits on individuals becoming physicians than there are for other allied medical professionals. This extends beyond simply the amount of time to complete the training. The number of training slots (both seats in domestic medical schools and residency slots at hospitals) are broadly fixed and limit expansions of the supply in response to changing economics. Similarly, physicians are highly trained individuals who may have far worse outside options in the labor market than practicing medicine. This could limit their willingness to move out of the labor force. In contrast, it is relatively less arduous to train for other medical occupations, and similar limitations do not exist constraining supply.

These different entry and exit barriers are important when considering the implications for understanding the potential impact of AI on the distribution of economic rents in the value chain. This is particularly true given the relatively fixed reimbursement of physicians over time that we discuss below.

1.7.3   Medical Malpractice Concerns[17]

A physician who makes an incorrect diagnosis or makes the wrong treatment recommendation, either of which resulting in harm to the patient, may be liable in court for damages and risk professional discipline.[18] This is true

---

17. Many of the concepts in this section are taken from Sullivan and Schweikart (2019)

18. The key cases are *Sarchett v. Blue Shield of California* 43 Cal. 3d 1, 233 Cal. Rptr. 76, 729 P. 2d 267, (1987) and *Wickline v. California* 192 Cal. App. 3d 1630, 239 Cal. Rptr. 810 (1986). Our discussion here draws on Gray and Field (1989).

even if the physician is following the recommendations of an informed third party, including government entities, such as Medicare-sponsored UR agencies, and private insurers. Physicians may also be liable if they implement suggestions developed through AI. This applies both when they perform services that proved to be medically unnecessary and when they failed to perform medically necessary procedures.

Case law suggests that physicians are ultimately liable for treatment decisions, even when third parties are involved. In *Sarchett v. Blue Shield of California*, the court affirmed the rights of third parties to disagree with a physician's diagnosis and determination of medical necessity. The court added, however, that any doubts about coverage should be construed in favor of the patient. In other words, if the physician insists that a procedure is medically necessary, the insurer should generally be required to cover it. While this seems to protect physicians, the subsequent *Wickline v. California* case limited that protection. The upshot of *Wickline* is that in situations where the physician deems a procedure is medically necessary but the payer denies coverage, both parties may be liable if failure to perform the procedure results in harm. In particular, the burden is on the physician to appeal the insurer's decision. At the same time, if the physician accepts the insurer's recommendation and something goes wrong, the physician is again liable. It seems that a physician who blindly accepts third-party oversight is inviting litigation.

It is not clear how these legal doctrines, which focus on human conduct, will apply to AI (Bathae 2018). As noted by Chinen (2016), "The more autonomy machines achieve, the more tenuous becomes the strategy of attributing and distributing legal responsibility for their behavior to human beings." Even if AI is held responsible (whatever that means), it could prove difficult to find a responsible party, as many individuals and companies contribute to the creation of AI systems. This could leave the physician as the only easily identifiable target in liability suits.[19] On the other hand, if the AI algorithm is developed in partnership with a health system, as is often the case, then plaintiffs will have a clearly identifiable and deep pocketed target.

Malpractice concerns do not entirely weigh against AI adoption. To the extent that AI improves the quality of third-party recommendations, it will reduce the malpractice risks inherent in the current system. Moreover, as much as physicians are at risk for following third-party recommendations that prove incorrect, they are also at risk if they fail to deliver medically necessary treatment or deliver what proves to be the objectively wrong treatment. As AI improves diagnostic accuracy and the appropriateness of treat-

---

19. It is worth adding that both the Employee Retirement Income Security Act of 1974 and various state doctrines effectively state that corporations cannot practice medicine and therefore cannot be liable for malpractice. (Trueman 2002).

ment recommendations, physicians can reduce their exposure to malpractice risk by following AI recommendations.

Concerns about medical malpractice could be exacerbated in a world where it is not entirely obvious how AI is making particular medical decisions without full knowledge of the process. Autor (2022) describes how we have moved from a world of Polanyi's paradox ("We do not know what we know) to Polanyi's revenge ("We do not know what the computer knows"). While there are a variety of tasks where the productivity gains are sufficient such that we may not care about this lack of knowledge, it is not clear that medical diagnoses and treatment falls in that category—particularly if physicians are worried that such a lack of knowledge could contribute to their liability in the event of a negative health outcome.

1.7.4   Resistance from Organized Medicine

As we discuss above, there is a long history of third-party intervention in medical decision making. When that intervention threatens physician discretion, as in 1990s-style UR, physicians and patients have openly resisted. Physicians are more receptive to advice from third parties, as with PORTS and evidence-based treatment protocols. When third parties partially base reimbursements on whether physicians follow that advice, the reaction has been mixed. This suggests physicians are likely to tolerate AI, provided it complements medical practice. AI that substitutes for physicians will be met with stubborn resistance. If the adoption of AI comes down to a battle between physicians and insurers, we suspect their role as a "trusted agent" will allow physicians to ultimately win. As in the past, insurers may limit using AI to dictate medical practice, and legislators may remove any malpractice exemptions for AI developers.

While resistance by organized medicine is often thought of as an impediment to the *adoption* of existing AI technologies, it is important to consider that in equilibrium the expectation of such resistance by the developers of technology would likely shape the very frontier of what comes to market. Without some amount of deliberate decision making by individuals both within and outside of the health care sector, the ability of value-creating technologies to enter the market in the face of such resistance and as a result society may fail to realize the full potential of AI for health care. This is also true to the degree that the optimal AI systems require meaningful interaction with medical practice to reach their full potential. In one way this is related to the development of such technologies. This, however, could be accomplished by a relatively small set of medical professionals who could have sufficient capital invested in the firms developing AI to overcome any financial resistance. It also could be that only through the adoption and iteration of technology across physicians without a financial stake in the process can we enjoy the most productive AI in health care. In those settings it may be hard to ever have AI reach its full potential.

1.7.5   Resistance from Patients

Perhaps the biggest reason for the managed care backlash of the 1990s was that consumers trusted their physicians more than their insurers. In particular, if payers dictated that particular tests were not medically or economically justifiable but physicians and patients desired such tests, there was little faith put into the "evidence-based medicine" recommended by the payers. There are certainly a number of reasons for this to occur. Part of this is the inherent trust in the physician that described by Arrow (1963). This trust has resulted in a fundamental belief that physicians are primarily interested in the health of their patients—an assertion that we do not contend with but that leaves an economically meaningful amount of "wiggle room" at the margin for medical procedures and tests that are financially advantageous to the physician without being overly injurious to the patient.

Another reason for the inherent distrust of insurers is that as the residual claimants on premiums not spent on medical services, they themselves have inherent economic biases to *undertreat* patients. In current settings, it is rare to see conflict between a physician and a payer be centered on the physician wanting a more conservative treatment path and the payer recommended more expensive and intensive treatments. However, in a world of expanded AI for medical decision making, such paths become more likely. This is particularly true in areas where physicians may have a higher rather of false negative diagnoses than a more automated system. It is unclear whether the emergence of such treatments would shift support away from physicians and toward payers.

One factor that may overcome provider and patient resistance to AI is the rapid evolution of payment modalities. Payers increasingly offer bonuses or in other ways tie compensation to cost savings and/or better outcomes. Payment reforms for hospitals are especially common, with many hospitals participating in accountable care organizations that allow the hospitals to share in any cost reductions, a far cry from fee-for-service and cost-based reimbursement methods common in the times of Arrow and Fuchs. Hospitals may find that following the dictates of AI allows them to enjoy large financial windfalls, and they may push the use of AI onto their doctors and allied medical staff. In this way, payers may indirectly impose the dictates of AI without necessarily feeling the same backlash.

1.8   AI and the Future of Physicians

We have argued that AI can either complement or substitute for labor. The labor economics literature contains a number of predictions about how the degree of complementarity versus substitution will impact the distribution of economic rents in the system. It is an open question beyond the scope of this paper or frankly our expertise as to what technologies will ultimately emerge. However, our analysis suggests that whether new technologies will be substitutes or complements depend on three factors:

1) The nature of the service—diagnosis versus clinical decision making
2) The extent to which physicians have access to information that is not available to or decipherable by a computer
3) The magnitude of biases in physician decision making

We lack the requisite medical knowledge to make definitive statements, but we can make some high-level observations. Regarding the nature of the service, the majority of published AI studies to date appear to target diagnostic accuracy. Studies suggest that AI produces sharply lower false negative and false positive rates, and at least one study shows that AI on its own outperforms physicians who incorporate AI into their final diagnosis. Given these facts, radiologists and pathologists—two relatively highly paid specialties—likely have a lot to fear from AI.

With regard to clinical decision making, there is likely to be a well-identified set of clinical conditions for which treatment recommendations can be standardized and for which physician expertise contributes little extra to value creation. Once patients with these conditions are identified, nurses or other allied medical personnel could issue treatment recommendations, as dictated by the AI system. The question is how to perform the necessary triage. In other words, someone has to obtain and enter the required information into the computer. It remains unclear whether physicians or other allied medical personnel will be better at soliciting such information from patients.

This brings us to the second consideration. When it comes to a computer issuing treatment recommendations, the old expression "Garbage in, garbage out" applies. We can imagine that there are some sets of symptoms and diagnostic test results that leave little margin for error. At the risk of proving our lack of medical knowledge, we suspect that conditions such as conjunctivitis (pink eye) or an ear infection are good examples. For patients presenting with the symptoms of these conditions, physician expertise is not required for the appropriate treatment recommendation. In fact, given concerns about the overuse of antibiotics, it is possible that having an unbiased and automated system may actually be superior in some of these situations.

At the other end of the spectrum are the array of rare diseases diagnosed by television character Dr. Gregory House, who frequently combined clues obtained from personal interactions with the patient and family with years of experience diagnosing rare conditions to make life-saving treatment recommendations. While this fictional character makes for an obvious extreme case, it is clear that value maximization by real world providers will continue to require careful judgments at the time patients present with symptoms and test results. After all, Polanyi's famous quote about the inability to explain what we know applies to patients as much as it does to the creators of automation. One important task of medical providers is the ability to elicit large amounts of information from patients and then determine what is important for the purpose of a medical diagnosis—some of which may be plainly obvious to a patient and some of which may only be apparent to a trained medical professional. For those specific symptoms and tests, it remains an open question as to whether these provider-patient interactions would be improved by the adoption of AI-based clinical decision making. In addition, given malpractice concerns, is it even possible that AI remains anything other than a complement to human medical decision making for all but the simplest clinical conditions?

We finally turn to third-party intervention into medical decision making. This has long been premised on the belief that physicians were biased in favor of performing too many unnecessary services. Even if physicians have information not available to the third party, such bias can justify limiting physician discretion. Utilization review and its descendants are just one way to address bias. In the past decade, payers have introduced a wide range of payment reforms that both limit incentives for overtreatment and reward providers for achieving quality metrics. AI offers an obvious alternative means of implementing more sophisticated means of UR. Again, considering the economic motivations of various actors here will be important. It is clear that a greater automation of UR will ease the burden on medical providers—an existing hassle cost that is a common lament of medical providers. What is unclear is whether that will be viewed as a positive for third-party payers. Given concerns that physicians may ultimately figure out how to "teach to the test" and provide an AI system with the information necessary to always receive approval for treatments, it may be that the cost of an arduous UR system is a feature and not a bug for the payer. That is to say, a higher cost for the physician may discipline how often the provider wants to seek additional treatments and ideally will cause the physician to sort these interactions based on the value created for the patient. While we admit that the current system may not be optimal, it is unclear that a new system relying on AI will be optimal given the economic incentives of the various parties in the value chain.

1.9 Value Capture by AI Developers

AI seems likely to affect value creation and value capture by physicians. In this section we explore the potential for AI developers to capture some of the value they create. We start with a simple observation: the AI market is highly fragmented. While IBM's Watson Health is the best-known AI vendor and IBM invested over $4 billion to build its health care capabilities,[20] it has generated no more than $1 billion in annual revenue and no profits.[21] At the same time, more than a dozen health care providers using IBM Watson

---

20. Reuters Staff, "IBM to Acquire Truven Health Analytics for $2.6 Billion," February 18, 2016, https://www.reuters.com/article/us-truven-m-a-ibm-idUSKCN0VR1SS.

21. Laura Cooper and Cara Lombardo, "IBM Explores Sale of IBM Watson Health," *Wall Street Journal*, February 18, 2021.

halted or reduced their oncology-related products, and there is little research evidence to show improvements in patient outcomes.[22] IBM sold the Watson Health unit to private equity firm Francisco Partners in 2022. Google Health was created in 2018 to consolidate that company's data-driven health care initiatives, which ranged from Google Brain (its AI initiative) to Fitbit. Google Health shut down after three years, with Google Brain moving into Google Research. Thus far, Google Brain has had little to show in terms of usable AI products in health care (or other sectors of the economy, for that matter.) The rest of AI development in health care is a hodgepodge of provider organizations, start-up tech companies, or joint ventures between the two.[23] By one count, health care accounts for a fifth of all venture funding in AI, and a recent publication highlighted forty start-ups from what is undoubtedly a much larger number.[24] To the extent that different companies are focusing on different areas of diagnosis and treatment, competition for AI products may be limited. That said, the market is likely to be fragmented for the foreseeable future.

At first blush, such fragmentation may seem surprising, given the obvious scale economies associated with data analytics. The history of the EHR market suggests otherwise. Hospitals began adopting advanced EHR systems, which include CDS, in the 2000s. The market was highly fragmented at first, but scale economies and network effects favored consolidation. The market has consolidated, yet remains only "moderately concentrated" (using merger guidelines), with leader Epic holding a 33 percent share of the hospital EHR market and the top four vendors (Epic, Cerner, Meditech, and CPSI) together holding 83 percent of the market.[25] Data on sales to physicians are harder to come by, but it appears that there are ten or more EHR companies for physicians.[26] While the reasons why the market has not further consolidated remains unclear, it does suggest that consolidation in the AI market might also be slow.

Why does fragmentation matter? Consider that most AI applications to date are developed through partnerships between AI developers and health care systems. Bearing in mind that competition among health care providers is local, a successful partnership should allow a local system to create more value. Back up the value chain to the beginning—where AI developers compete to partner with the local system—and we see that fragmentation

22. Daniela Hernandez and Ted Greenwald, "IBM Has a Watson Dilemma," *Wall Street Journal*, August 11, 2018.

23. For further discussion of AI start-ups, see Bertalan Mesko, "Top Artificial Intelligence Companies in Healthcare to Keep and Eye On," *The Medical Futurist*, January 19, 2023, https://medicalfuturist.com/top-artificial-intelligence-companies-in-healthcare/#.

24. See https://builtin.com/artificial-intelligence/artificial-intelligence-healthcare. Accessed August 10, 2022.

25. See https://www.beckershospitalreview.com/ehrs/ehr-vendors-ranked-by-percentage-of-hospital-market-share.html. Accessed August 3, 2022.

26. See https://www.praxisemr.com/top-ehr-vendors.html. Accessed August 3, 2022.

among developers would force them to compete away their rents, leaving them to local providers. To the extent that the local provider market is also fragmented, the health systems will themselves compete away their rents, leaving patients to enjoy the lion's share of benefits.

Consolidation of the AI market would change the calculus of value capture. This calculus also changes to the extent that AI developers and health care providers form deep partnerships with substantial specific investments. Learning distinct data systems and earning the trust of physicians can take time. A developer that embeds itself in a health system stands to capture a sizable portion of the value it creates.

1.10   AI in Less Developed Economic Settings

Much of the discussion of AI in this paper (and in the existing literature) has focused on its adoption in developed country markets and its interaction with the economic incentives of medical provider and third-party payers in those markets. We would be remiss, however, not to also discuss the vastly different implications of a widespread use of AI in less economically developed settings—particularly those without meaningful access to trained medical providers. After all, it is one thing to debate whether AI is superior to a physician alone, an affiliated medical provider working with AI, or some other combination of trained inputs. It is quite another when the counterfactual is no treatment or diagnosis at all—which sadly remains the case in many developing countries. These considerations can also influence discussions about the optimal organization of medical markets in rural settings of developed countries such as the United States—which also often lack ready access to specialists of all types.

In cases where access to medical professionals is constrained and it is not immediately obvious how to relax such constraints, there could be very different welfare implications of even relatively poorly performing automation. After all, in such settings it is not obvious automation should be evaluated against a hypothetical ideal medical diagnosis but instead against a realistic counterfactual of the available standard of care.

That said, as we consider the incentives of the developers of AI, it is possible that the very economic institutions that constrain the availability of medical providers may decrease the economic value of AI to firms developing such technologies. Consider the case of the biopharmaceutical industry, which develops products using a market-based, for-profit model. Under such a model a host of medical conditions endemic to developing countries, such as malaria and other neglected tropical diseases, remain underinvestigated. This is not because of a lack of social value—after all over 400,000 individuals die each year from malaria. Instead, this lack of investment stems directly from the inability of firms to capture a sufficient amount of the social value that they create.

Could AI for developing countries suffer the same fate? It is possible that there are a host of automated technologies that could develop meaningful value in rural or developing country settings but remain overlooked because of the lack of a reasonable expectation of reimbursement by innovators.

Solutions to this possibility are not immediately obvious. While there is a role for government or nongovernmental organizations to step into this area, it is not clear for political economy reasons that we will see such actions. It is one thing for a philanthropy to propose funding a cure for currently incurable condition; it is another to offer funding for an AI system that would not be implemented in a developed market but offers superior efficacy to the existing conditions in a less developed market.

1.11   Conclusion

As the technological frontier advances, the possibility for AI to generate meaningful economic value increases. While this is true for the entire economy, we highlight a series of unique features in the health care sector that would change some implications and predictions for technology in this sector.

While it is well beyond our expertise to predict the future of what technologies can emerge, economics offers important insights into the impact of certain types of technology on market actors. Understanding how the potential emergence of AI can alter the existing distribution of economic surplus in the value chain is important for both predicting and managing the impact of this technology. This is true for allocators of capital and policymakers alike.

It is clear there is great potential for AI to create welfare across a variety of health care settings in developed and developing countries. However, this impact will be a function of exactly which technologies are both developed and adopted. A particularly important point is for actors from outside of health care to understand how the incentives of existing medical providers can influence the future of AI. This could highlight areas where a greater degree of intervention from outside of the sector may be warranted.

References

Acemoglu, Daron, and Pascual Restrepo. 2020. "Robots and Jobs: Evidence from US Labor Markets." *Journal of Political Economy* 128 (6): 2188–244.
Alkhaldi, Nadejda. 2021. "Artificial Intelligence in Radiology—Use Cases and Trends." Ritrex Strategy. June 9, 2021. https://itrexgroup.com/blog/artificial-intelligence-in-radiology-use-cases-predictions/#header.
American College of Surgeons. 1982. *Second Surgical Opinion Programs: A Review and Progress Report*. Chicago: American College of Surgeons.

Arrow, Kenneth J. 1963. "Uncertainty and the Welfare Economics of Medical Care." *American Economic Review* 53 (5): 941–73.

Autor, David H. 2014. "Skills, Education, and the Rise of Earnings Inequality among the 'Other 99 Percent.'" *Science* 344 (6186): 843–51.

Autor, David. 2022. *The Labor Market Impacts of Technological Change: From Unbridled Enthusiasm to Qualified Optimism to Vast Uncertainty*. NBER Working Paper No. 30074. Cambridge, MA: National Bureau of Economic Research.

Autor, David H., Frank Levy, and Richard J. Murnane. 2003. "The Skill Content of Recent Technological Change: An Empirical Exploration." *Quarterly Journal of Economics* 118 (4): 1279–333.

Bathae, Yavar. 2018. "The Artificial Intelligence Black Box and the Failure of Intent and Causation." *Harvard Journal of Law & Technology* 31 (2): 889–938.

Chandra, Amitabh, and Douglas O. Staiger. 2007. "Productivity Spillovers in Health Care: Evidence from the Treatment of Heart Attacks." *Journal of Political Economy* 115 (1): 103–40.

Chinen, Mark A. 2016. "The Co-evolution of Autonomous Machines and Legal Responsibility." *Virginia Journal of Law & Technology* 20 (2): 338–93.

Clemens, Jeffrey, Joshua D. Gottlieb, and Tímea Laura Molnár. 2017. "Do Health Insurers Innovate? Evidence from the Anatomy of Physician Payments." *Journal of Health Economics* 55: 153–67.

Croskerry, Pat. 2018. "Adaptive Expertise in Medical Decision Making." *Medical Teacher* 40 (8): 803–8.

Cutler, David, Jonathan S. Skinner, Ariel Dora Stern, and David Wennberg. 2019. "Physician Beliefs and Patient Preferences: A New Look at Regional Variation in Health Care Spending." *American Economic Journal: Economic Policy* 11 (1): 192–221.

Dranove, David. 1988. "Demand Inducement and the Physician/Patient Relationship." *Economic Inquiry* 26 (2): 281–98.

Dranove, David. 1993. "The Five Ws of Utilization Review." In *American Health Policy: Critical Issues for Reform*, edited by Robert B. Helms. Washington, DC: American Enterprise Institute.

Eijkenaar, Frank, Martin Emmert, Manfred Scheppach, and Oliver Schöffski. 2013. "Effects of Pay for Performance in Health Care: A Systematic Review of Systematic Reviews." *Health Policy* 110 (2–3): 115–30.

Evans, Robert G. 1974. "Supplier-Induced Demand: Some Empirical Evidence and Implications." In *The Economics of Health and Medical Care*, ed. Mark Perlman, 162–73. London: Palgrave Macmillan.

Finkelstein, Amy, Matthew Gentzkow, and Heidi Williams. 2016. "Sources of Geographic Variation in Health Care: Evidence from Patient Migration." *Quarterly Journal of Economics* 131 (4): 1681–726.

Freund, Deborah, Judith Lave, Carolyn Clancy, Gillian Hawker, Victor Hasselblad, Robert Keller, Ellen Schneiter, and James Wright.. 1999. "Patient Outcomes Research Teams: Contribution to Outcomes and Effectiveness Research." *Annual Reviews of Public Health* 20: 337–59.

Fuchs, Victor R. 1974. *Who Shall Live? Health, Economics and Social Choice*. Singapore: World Scientific.

Fuchs, Victor R. 1978. "The Supply of Surgeons and the Demand for Operations." NBER Working Paper No. 236. Cambridge, MA: National Bureau of Economic Research.

Gallup Survey. 2022. "Honesty/Ethics in Professions." Accessed August 5, 2022. https://news.gallup.com/poll/1654/Honesty-Ethics-Professions.aspx

Gottlieb, Joshua D., Maria Polyakova, Kevin Rinz, Hugh Shiplett, and Victoria Udalova. 2020. "Who Values Human Capitalists' Human Capital?: Healthcare

Spending and Physician Earnings." US Census Bureau, Center for Economic Studies, Working Paper No. CES-20-23.

Gray, Bradford H., and Marilyn J. Field, eds. 1989. *Controlling Costs and Changing Patient Care? The Role of Utilization Management*. Washington, DC: National Academies Press.

Hilzenrath, David S. 1997. "Backlash Builds Over Managed Care." *Washington Post*, June 30, A01.

Hollon, Todd C., Balaji Pandian, Arjun R. Adapa, Esteban Urias, Akshay V. Save, Siri Sahib S. Khalsa, Daniel G. Eichberg, et al. 2020. "Near Real-Time Intraoperative Brain Tumor Diagnosis Using Stimulated Raman Histology and Deep Neural Networks." *Nature Medicine* 26 (1): 52–58.

Hosny, Ahmed, Chintan Parmar, John Quackenbush, Lawrence H. Schwartz, and Hugo J. W. L. Aerts. 2018. "Artificial Intelligence in Radiology." *Nature Reviews Cancer* 18 (8): 500–510.

Interqual. 1989. *The ISD-A Review System with Adult Criteria: Consultants, Educators and Publishers to Healthcare Providers*. North Hampton, NH: Interqual.

Jing, Bocheng, W. John Boscardin, W. James Deardorff, Sun Young Jeon, Alexandra K. Lee, Anne L. Donovan, and Sei J. Lee. 2022. "Comparing Machine Learning to Regression Methods for Mortality Prediction Using Veterans Affairs Electronic Health Record Clinical Data." *Medical Care* 60 (6): 470–79.

Kim, Hyo-Eun, Hak Hee Kim, Boo-Kyung Han, Ki Hwan Kim, Kyunghwa Han, Hyeonseob Nam, Eun Hye Lee, and Eun-Kyung Kim.. 2020. "Changes in Cancer Detection and False-Positive Recall in Mammography Using Artificial Intelligence: A Retrospective, Multireader Study." *Lancet Digital Health* 2 (3): e138–e148.

Kohn, Linda T., Janet M. Corrigan, and Moola S. Donaldson, eds. 2000. *To Err Is Human: Building a Safer Health System*. Washington, DC: National Academy Press

Lee, Aaron Y., Ryan T. Yanagihara, Cecilia S. Lee, Marian Blazes, Hoon C. Jung, Yewlin E. Chee, Michael D. Gencarella, Harry Gee, April Y. Maa, Glenn C. Cockerham, Mary Lynch, and Edward J. Boyko. 2021. "Multicenter, Head-to-Head, Real-World Validation Study of Seven Automated Artificial Intelligence Diabetic Retinopathy Screening Systems." *Diabetes Care* 44 (5): 1168–175.

Luft, Harold S. 1978. "How Do Health-Maintenance Organizations Achieve Their 'Savings'?" *New England Journal of Medicine* 298 (24): 1336–43.

Mawatari, Tsubasa, Yoshiko Hayashida, Shigehiko Katsuragawa, Yuta Yoshimatsu, Toshihiko Hamamura, Kenta Anai, Midori Ueno, Satoru Yamaga, Issei Ueda, Takashi Terasawa, Akitaka Fujisaki, Chihiro Chihara, Tomoyuki Miyagi, Takatoshi Aoki, and Yukunori Korogi. 2020. "The Effect of Deep Convolutional Neural Networks on Radiologists' Performance in the Detection of Hip Fractures on Digital Pelvic Radiographs." *European Journal of Radiology* 130: 109188.

Mullainathan, Sendhil, and Ziad Obermeyer. 2021. "Diagnosing Physician Error: A Machine Learning Approach to Low-Value Health Care." *Quarterly Journal of Economics* 137 (2): 679–727.

Obermeyer, Ziad, Brian Powers, Christine Vogeli, and Sendhil Mullainathan. 2019. "Dissecting Racial Bias in an Algorithm Used to Manage the Health of Populations." *Science* 366 (6464): 446–53.

Olmstead, Alan L., and Paul W. Rhode. 2001. "Reshaping the Landscape: The Impact and Diffusion of the Tractor in American Agriculture, 1910–1960." *Journal of Economic History* 61 (3): 663–98.

Patel, Nirali M., Vanessa V. Michelini, Jeff M. Snell, Saianand Balu, Alan P. Hoyle, Joel S. Parker, Michele C. Hayward, et al. 2018. "Enhancing Next-Generation

Sequencing-Guided Cancer Care through Cognitive Computing." *Oncologist* 23 (2): 179–85.

Piette, John D., Sarah L Krein, Dana Striplin, Nicolle Marinec, Robert D Kerns, Karen B Farris, Satinder Singh, Lawrence An, and Alicia A Heapy. 2016. "Patient-Centered Pain Care Using Artificial Intelligence and Mobile Health Tools: Protocol for a Randomized Study Funded by the US Department of Veterans Affairs Health Services Research and Development Program." *JMIR Research Protocols* 5 (2): e53.

Rasmussen, Wayne D. 1982. "The Mechanization of Agriculture." *Scientific American* 247 (3): 76–89.

Rodriguez-Diaz, Eladio, György Baffy, Wai-Kit Lo, Hiroshi Mashimo, Gitanjali Vidyarthi, Shyam S. Mohapatra, and Satish K. Singh.. 2021. "Real-Time Artificial Intelligence–Based Histologic Classification of Colorectal Polyps with Augmented Visualization." *Gastrointestinal Endoscopy* 93 (3): 662–70.

Roemer, Milton I. 1961. "Bed Supply and Hospital Utilization: A Natural Experiment." *Hospitals* 35: 36–42.

Shain, Max, and Milton I. Roemer. 1959. "Hospital Costs Relate to the Supply of Beds." *Journal of Occupational and Environmental Medicine* 1 (9): 518.

Sullivan, Hannah R., and Scott J. Schweikart. 2019. "Are Current Tort Liability Doctrines Adequate for Addressing Injury Caused by AI?" *AMA Journal of Ethics* 21 (2): 160–66.

Susskind, Daniel. 2020. *A World without Work: Technology, Automation and How We Should Respond.* London: Penguin.

Tschider, C. 2019. "The Healthcare Privacy-Artificial Intelligence Impasse." *Santa Clara High Technology Law Journal* 36 (4): 439.

Toner, R. 2001. "Debate on Patients' Rights Sends Lobbyists into Battle." *New York Times*, June 20, Section A, Page 1.

Trueman, D. 2002. "The Liability of Medical Directors for Utilization Review Decisions." *Journal of Health Law* 35 (1): 105–43.

Wennberg, John, and Alan Gittelsohn. 1973. "Small Area Variations in Health Care Delivery: A Population-Based Health Information System Can Guide Planning and Regulatory Decision-Making." *Science* 182 (4117): 1102–8.

Wickizer, Thomas M. 1990. "The Effect of Utilization Review on Hospital Use and Expenditures: A Review of the Literature and an Update on Recent Findings." *Medical Care Review* 47 (3): 327–63.

Wickizer, Thomas M., John R. C. Wheeler, and Paul J. Feldstein 1989. "Does Utilization Review Reduce Unnecessary Care and Contain Costs?" *Medical Care* 27 (6): 632–46.

Wickizer, Thomas M., and Daniel Lessler. 2002. "Utilization Management: Issues, Effects, and Future Prospects." *Annual Review of Public Health* 23: 233–54.

Comment   Dawn Bell

Dranove and Garthwaite hypothesize that artificial intelligence can either be a substitute or a complement for medical decision making. They provide a useful history of efforts to improve medical decision making over the past 60+ years, focusing on resource utilization management schemes including mandatory second opinions, utilization review, and clinical practice guidelines (all of which have had varying success). What has remained unchanged is the central and persistent role of physicians in medical decision making and the continuing desire to improve the quality of their decisions while controlling costs of healthcare utilization.

The past decades have seen a "protocolization" of many areas of health care as evidence-based medicine has gained momentum and large-scale randomized clinical trials have become standard for the adoption and approval of important medical interventions. This phenomenon is revealed in the increasing prevalence of clinical practice guidelines, a codified standard of practice for various conditions ranging from diabetes mellitus to cardiovascular disease to diagnosis and management of common cancers. While adherence to clinical practice guideline recommendations is uneven, this is largely believed to be an issue of poor implementation rather than disagreement of the medical standards codified in the documents themselves. So, while physicians remain resistant to some forms of influence over their decision-making autonomy, there are areas where they adapt their behaviors to an agreed standard. This is good news for the adoption of AI, as clinical practice guidelines are an analogue analog to AI algorithms. But for reasons clearly pointed out in the paper, there are many barriers to AI adoption and progress is likely to be slow, fragmented, and inefficient. Nevertheless, adoption of AI in healthcare is increasing and will continue to increase. It is unlikely to replace physicians, but will replace many routine activities and may replace some high-value activities currently performed by some physicians.

The adoption of AI in healthcare can be likened to the evolution of autonomous vehicles. As drivers, we first gave up our maps and adopted GPS. The first step in codifying clinical decision making—clinical practice guidelines—can be compared to early GPS devices (think of the Garmin). It wasn't integrated into driving workflows, and was clunky and not all that easy to use. But GPS improved and has been widely adopted. It was integrated into most new cars and evolved to be adaptive (e.g., Waze). Health

Dawn Bell is global head of strategic partnerships in the Research and Development Division of Novartis.

For acknowledgments, sources of research support, and disclosure of the author's material financial relationships, if any, please see https://www.nber.org/books-and-chapters/economics-artificial-intelligence-health-care-challenges/impact-artificial-intelligence-cost-and-quality-medical-decision-making-bell.

systems are integrating AI-enabled decision support systems into their EHRs and workflows in a similar way.

Then cars started getting better at helping drivers drive safely—sensors and cameras to help you park, alert you when you are about to swerve out of your lane, or give a signal if you are getting too close to the car in front of you or an object behind you. And then cars got even better. They can now parallel park for you, do lane corrections to prevent drift or swerving, and apply the brakes if you are getting too close—these features are accepted and welcome additions to "safe driving." The modern automobile helps today's drivers much like AI decision support products can assist physicians and other medical professionals with higher-quality decision making. And while we know some cars can drive you home already, as a society we just aren't quite ready to take our hands off the wheel.

The same is true of AI in healthcare. Products viewed by physicians as helping them make better decisions and allowing them to delegate "routine" care to midlevel providers will mostly be welcomed (and have been implemented in some situations). As AI becomes more reliable and the medical community becomes more comfortable with it, what is specialized care today will become the routine care of tomorrow, improving the quality of medical decision making in the process. This is all good news for patients who suffer most from errors in physician judgement and under- and overutilization of medical resources. We don't need to concern ourselves with replacing physicians just yet—let's just work on getting all of them to play at the top of their game.

The Potential Impact of Artificial Intelligence on Health Care Spending

Nikhil R. Sahni, George Stein, Rodney Zemmel, and David Cutler

2.1 Introduction

Can artificial intelligence (AI) improve productivity in health care? That is a central question in the United States and the focus of this paper.

In the United States, health care is considered too expensive for what it delivers. Businesses are looking to manage their costs, and health care spending is a large and growing expense. As health care spending grows in the public sector, it crowds out other governmental budget priorities. Previous research has found that health care in the United States could be more productive—both costing less and delivering better care (Berwick and Hackbarth 2012; Sahni et al. 2019). AI is likely to be part of the solution.

The improvement in US health care productivity could manifest in several ways. Administrative costs are estimated to account for nearly 25 percent of all US health care spending (Sahni et al. 2021); AI could reduce this burden. Harnessing clinical knowledge to improve patient health is a second way. Medical knowledge is growing so rapidly that only 6 percent of what the average new physician is taught at medical school today will be relevant

Nikhil R. Sahni is a partner and leader of McKinsey's Center of US Healthcare Improvement at McKinsey & Company and a fellow in the Economics Department of Harvard University.

George Stein is an associate partner at McKinsey & Company.

Rodney Zemmel is a senior partner and global leader of McKinsey Digital at McKinsey & Company.

David Cutler is the Otto Eckstein Professor of Applied Economics at Harvard University and a research associate of the National Bureau of Economic Research.

This paper was prepared for the NBER Economics of Artificial Intelligence Conference, September 2022. The paper represents the views of the authors and not any entity with which they may be affiliated. For acknowledgments, sources of research support, and disclosure of the authors' material financial relationships, if any, please see https://www.nber.org/books-and-chapters/economics-artificial-intelligence-health-care-challenges/potential-impact-artificial-intelligence-healthcare-spending.

in ten years (Rajkomar, Dean, and Kohane 2019). Technology such as AI could provide valuable clinical data to the clinician at the time of diagnosis. Improving clinical operations is still another example. Operating rooms (ORs) are one of hospitals' most critical assets. Yet inefficient operations can result in wasted hours, leading to excessive building of space, hindering patient access, degrading the patient experience, and reducing hospitals' financial margins.

In this paper we focus on two questions about AI. First, how much might be saved by wider adoption of AI in health care? To answer this, we estimate potential savings by considering how AI might affect processes for three stakeholder groups—hospitals, physician groups, and private payers. For each stakeholder group, we illustrate AI-enabled use cases across both medical and administrative costs and review case studies. Using national health care spending data, we then scale the estimates to the entire US health care industry. We find that AI adoption within the next five years using today's technologies could result in savings of 5 to 10 percent of health care spending, or $200 billion to $360 billion annually in 2019 dollars, without sacrificing quality and access.[1] For hospitals, the savings come largely from use cases that improve clinical operations (for example, OR optimization) and quality and safety (for example, condition deterioration management or adverse event detection). For physician groups, the savings also mostly come from use cases that improve clinical operations (for example, capacity management) and continuity of care (for example, referral management). For private payers, the savings come largely from use cases that improve claims management (for example, auto-adjudication or prior authorization), health care management (for example, tailored care management or avoidable readmissions), and provider relationship management (for example, network design or provider directory management). While we only quantify cost savings in this paper, there are additional nonfinancial benefits from the adoption of AI, including improved health care quality, increased access, better patient experience, and greater clinician satisfaction.

The magnitude of these savings raises a second question: If AI in health care can be so valuable, why is it not in greater use? At the organizational level, in our experience, there are six factors for successful AI adoption. AI's limited uptake can be partly explained by the difficulty of addressing these factors, such as the failure to create "digital trust" with patients. In addition, we discuss industry-level challenges such as data heterogeneity, lack of patient confidence, and misaligned incentives. Recent market trends, such as

---

1. In this paper, we focus only on what is possible using existing technologies. The opportunity increases as more advanced approaches come to market, such as digital twins or generative AI. We also acknowledge the adoption of AI elsewhere in the health care value chain, from medical training to pharmaceutical discovery to medical device manufacturing, none of which are discussed in this paper.

increasing venture capital and private equity investments, may increase the rate of AI adoption in the near future.

The paper is organized as follows. Section 2.2 outlines the scope of potential uses of AI in health care. Section 2.3 lays out how AI might be used for the three specific stakeholder groups—hospitals, physician groups, and private payers—and presents case studies as examples. Section 2.4 estimates the annual net savings that might result from adopting AI across all of US health care. Section 2.5 considers the challenges to greater adoption of AI, and section 2.6 discusses how market trends may change the decisions that organizations make about adopting AI. The final section offers concluding thoughts.

We note that the authors of this paper are an unusual group compared with the authors of other economics papers. One of the authors is an academic, and three are consultants with extensive experience in health care. Thus, our insights draw upon a combination of academic and industry experience. In many cases, the insights are not based on randomized control trials or quasi-experimental evidence; rather, they are distillations of observations from a number of organizations, in and out of health care. Given this, the reader should understand that the evidence base underpinning some of our conclusions is less analytically rigorous than traditional economics papers.

2.2   The Scope of AI

We define AI as a machine or computing platform capable of making intelligent decisions. Health care has more often pursued two types of AI: machine learning (ML), which involves computational techniques that learn from examples rather than operating from predefined rules; and natural language processing (NLP), which is a computer's ability to understand human language and transform unstructured text into machine-readable, structured data. An example of ML is recommending additional purchases based on a consumer's current choices, such as a book or a shirt; an example of NLP is analyzing written customer feedback to identify trends in sentiment that can inform improvements in a product's features.

It is not hard to envision the application of these technologies to health care. ML examples include predicting whether a patient is likely to be readmitted to a hospital, using remote patient monitoring to predict whether a patient's condition may deteriorate, optimizing clinician staffing levels in a hospital to match patient demand, and assisting in interpreting images and scans. NLP examples include extracting words from clinician notes to complete a chart or assign codes; translating a clinician's spoken words into notes; filling the role of a virtual assistant to communicate with a patient, help them check their symptoms, and direct them to the right channel such as a telemedicine visit or a phone call; and analyzing calls to route members to the right resource and to identify the most common call inquiries. Sometimes combining ML and NLP can create greater value; for example, using NLP to extract clinician notes and then using ML to predict whether a prior authorization is needed.

In general, AI-enabled use cases address operational processes. One type of operational change is simplifying an existing process. In these situations, the ideal processes usually are repetitive in nature, are highly manual, or involve complex decision trees. For example, forecasting inventory, demand, and capacity in the manufacturing, retail, and hospitality industries was once a highly manual job, involving meticulous note taking and trend forecasts. AI can perform the same processes faster with more precision. Another type of operational change is the creation of new processes. These generally were not accessible to organizations until now, but AI has unlocked them. For example, some insurance companies allow customers to send a photo of an incident to initiate a claim, which is then automatically processed by AI.

The application of AI in these use cases allows value to be created in several ways. Labor productivity improvement is one of the most important levers in health care. Historically, labor productivity growth in health care has been negative; only education has performed worse among all US services industries over the past few decades (Sahni et al. 2019). For many health care organizations, labor represents the single largest variable-cost item. Value can also be created in nonfinancial ways. For example, furnishing clinicians with data at the point of service could improve the course of treatment selected for the patient based on clinical evidence. As a result, health outcomes may improve with no increase—or even a reduction—in costs.

Adopting AI to create this value would unlock multiple levels of potential automation in health care. We illustrate these by considering the current use of AI in autonomous cars (figure 2.1). The Society of Automotive Engineers defines five levels of automation (Society of Automotive Engineers 2021). Each increasing level involves a greater degree of autonomous input: no driving automation but automatic emergency procedures in level 0, driver assistance such as lane centering in level 1, partial automation such as adaptive cruise control in level 2, conditional driving automation such as in traffic jams in level 3, local driverless taxis in level 4, and anywhere driverless taxis in level 5. At level 3 and above, the technology is in greater control than the human.

It is difficult to align on a single level for all of health care because AI-enabled use cases may vary. For example, clinical decision making is likely to approach level 1: the clinician makes final decisions jointly with the patient, but AI acts as a "member of the team" to present possible courses of treatments. The interpretation of radiology images could exemplify level 2, with AI reviewing an MRI or X-ray and outputting an interpretation. Humans would make the final decision for quality control and ensure the AI algorithm is trained properly. AI-enabled use cases in which technology would

	Human-led			Technology-led		
Level	**0**	**1**	**2**	**3**	**4**	**5**
Description	No driving automation	Driver assistance	Partial driving automation	Conditional driving automation	High driving automation	Full driving automation
Example driving features (Automotive)	Automatic emergency braking	Lane centering	Lane centering *and* adaptative cruise control at the same time	Traffic jam chauffeur	Local driverless taxi	Anywhere driverless taxi
Example AI-enabled use cases (Healthcare)	N/A	Clinical decision making	Interpreting radiology images	Referral recommenda-tions	Claims automation	

Most likely level of automation for healthcare AI-enabled use cases

Fig. 2.1   Society of Automotive Engineers levels of automation adapted to health care
Source: Society of Automotive Engineers 2021; authors' analysis

play the leading role could include referral recommendations (level 3) and claims automation (level 4).

2.3   Domains of AI in Health Care

To understand how AI might influence health care spending, we start by breaking down the industry into five stakeholder groups—hospitals, physician groups, private payers, public payers, and other sites of care, such as dentists and home health.[2] We focus primarily on the first three, which collectively represent 80 percent of total industry revenue (Singhal and Patel 2022).

For each of these stakeholder groups, we identify the key domains with underlying AI-enabled use cases. A "domain" is defined as a core functional focus area for an organization. A "use case" is a discrete process that is addressed within a domain. For example, hospitals have clinical operations teams (a domain) that specialize in operating room efficiency (a use case). For each domain, we consider whether the use of AI will affect medical or administrative costs. We also note the position of each domain along the adoption curve. We define this as a typical technology S-curve—first developing solutions, then piloting, followed by scaling and adapting, and finally reaching maturity. In addition, we identify whether the processes affected are existing or new.

In addition, we provide a measure of impact on "total mission value." Health Care involves many nonfinancial factors, such as quality outcomes,

---

2. We recognize that many hospitals are part of broader health systems. In this paper, we use the term *hospital* to reference just that portion of a broader health system when applicable.

patient safety, patient experience, clinician satisfaction, and access to care. The combination of financial and nonfinancial factors is what we term total mission value.

2.3.1   Hospitals

2.3.1.1   Domain Breakdown

In our experience, AI-enabled use cases are emerging in nine domains: continuity of care, network and market insights, clinical operations, clinical analytics, quality and safety, value-based care, reimbursement, corporate functions, and consumer (figure 2.2).[3] Within clinical operations, for example, hospitals are focusing on use cases such as improving the capacity of the operating room, freeing up clinical staff time, and optimizing the supply chain (Luo et al. 2020; Kilic et al. 2020). Clinical analytics, with AI-enabled use cases such as clinical decision making or treatment recommendations, is another area of focus for hospitals, usually within specialties such as radiology (Allen et al. 2021). A key domain, and the focus of much academic research, is quality and safety. This includes AI-enabled use cases such as predicting the likelihood of condition deterioration, an adverse event, or a readmission (Bates et al. 2021).

Some domains, such as reimbursement and corporate functions, are more advanced in AI adoption than others. Key reasons for the variation in uptake among hospitals include organizational priority and need, availability of data, and the share of AI deployment in the total budget.

Consider the quality and safety domain. There have been only a few successful use cases, such as identifying sepsis early or the prediction of adverse events (Bates et al. 2021; Nemati et al. 2018; Cooley-Rieders and Zheng 2021). This is due in part to the need for a strong business case to launch a pilot. When an organization considers only financial factors, AI-enabled use cases usually do not meet the threshold for investment. The business cases for adopting AI become more compelling when the focus shifts to total mission value, which includes nonfinancial factors such as experience and access.

Five domains have a greater impact on administrative costs than on medical costs: continuity of care, network and market insights, value-based care, reimbursement, and corporate functions. These are further along in part because administrative costs are generally associated with processes that that are manual and repetitive, which AI is well suited to address. However, the overall opportunity is likely lower given that administrative costs represent a smaller portion of the total than medical costs do.

---

3. The consumer domain is not included in our estimates because AI-enabled use cases in this domain often lead to a zero-sum outcome between hospitals. Revenue for one organization is generally taken from another organization.

Domain	Description	Examples of AI-enabled use cases	Potential impact on total mission value[1]	Position on technology adoption curve[2]	Cost category affected[3]	Process type affected
Continuity of care	Optimizing point-of-service and referrals to improve patient care	Referral management; Patient transfers			Admin	Existing
Network and market insights	Tracking relationship strength among providers	Provider segmentation; Benchmarking (e.g., quality, cost effectiveness)		P	Admin	Existing
Clinical operations	Optimizing clinical workflow and capacity throughout care journey	Operations optimization (e.g., ED, OR, units)[4]; Capacity/bed management; Supply chain optimization		P	Medical	Existing
Clinical analytics	Improving patient care journey with data at all points of care delivery	Clinical decision support; Treatment recommendations; Care pathway design		P	Medical	New
Quality and safety	Reducing major adverse events with special attention to patient experience and legal compliance	Condition deterioration; Readmissions; Regulatory compliance		D	Medical	New
Value-based care	Improving patient outcomes with value-based care models	Patient stratification and risk scoring; Utilization management		P	Medical	New
Reimbursement	Automating and optimizing payment flows between providers and payers	Coding; Denials management		S	Admin	Existing
Corporate functions	Managing back-office, administrative functions	Talent management; Call center enablement		S	Admin	Existing
Consumer	Understanding how best to engage consumers using tools	Segmentation and channel preference; Personalized engagement	Not included in sizing given use cases often are a net-zero activity across entities			

Fig. 2.2 Hospital AI domains and example use cases

1. We define "total mission value" as the combination of financial and nonfinancial factors, such as quality outcomes, patient safety, patient experience, clinician satisfaction, and access to care.

2. D = development of solutions; P = piloting; S = scaling and adapting; M = mature.

3. Positioning represents the direct cost category affected; second order effects may also reduce costs, but are not estimated.

4. ED = emergency department; OR = operating room.

Source: Authors' analysis

2.3.1.2   Case Study in Corporate Functions

During the COVID-19 pandemic, one multistate hospital's call center experienced a large increase in call volumes as patients sought more information on topics such as billing, COVID-19 tests, COVID-19 vaccines, scheduling and finding a clinician, searching for care, and getting a telemedicine visit. The hospital had not anticipated the increase in call volumes and was not staffed accordingly; nor did it have adequate existing call routing protocols. As a result, the hospital observed higher call wait times and dropped calls, both of which negatively affected patient experience and access to care.

Using NLP, which is well suited for tasks that have a consistent set of outcomes, the hospital created a virtual agent (a digital version of a customer service representative) for its mobile app and website. This virtual agent would answer common questions and route patient questions to a specific, prebuilt process with the appropriate supporting information. As a result of this rollout, call volume decreased by nearly 30 percent, the patient experience improved, and managers redeployed workers to less manual, more customized tasks such as answering calls related to upcoming and completed procedures.

2.3.1.3   Case Study in Clinical Operations

One large regional hospital was losing surgical volumes to other local hospitals. The surgical team investigated the OR schedule and found that while ORs appeared to be 100 percent blocked, actual utilization was about 60 percent. Reasons for this underuse included historical block-scheduling techniques that did not adjust time allocation based on surgeon demand, scheduled time slot durations that did not reflect actual surgical times (for example, some operations were scheduled for longer than they actually took, leaving unused time), and manual processes related to the release and reallocation of unused blocks.

Hospital leadership and frontline managers used AI to optimize the OR block scheduler—the system for assigning surgical time slots to surgeons—for more than 25 ORs and dozens of surgeons. An AI algorithm ingested historical block utilization and trends; forecast case hours by specialty, physician group, or surgeon; and rules related to procedural equipment needs, staffing, and surgeon availability. An optimization algorithm was then run to generate proposed schedules for a given week, using current schedules as a reference. To ensure acceptance of the results, the hospital worked with surgeons throughout the process, incorporating their insights into the algorithms. The solution has increased the amount of open time in the OR schedule by 30 percent, making it easier to treat patients with critical needs sooner. To sustain this progress, a data scientist was assigned responsibility for the algorithm and provides ongoing review of the output with the OR team for continued buy-in.

2.3.2   Physician Groups

2.3.2.1   Domain Breakdown

For physician groups, AI-enabled use cases are developing in the same nine domains as hospitals (figure 2.3). Within clinical operations, physician groups aim to reduce missed visits (patients failing to show up for a planned appointment) and ensure access to procedures by focusing on overall workflow, operations, access, and care team deployment. For example, understanding which patients might miss an appointment or need support with transportation influences how the clinical team conducts outreach to patients and the overall schedule of the physician group. Quality and safety is another domain of focus, especially for physician groups in value-based arrangements, where quality and safety outcomes directly affect financial performance. For example, AI supporting a value-based arrangement may predict which patients are at higher risk for readmission, therefore enabling care team members to intervene and address a patient's care needs to prevent deterioration in the condition. As these payment models grow in acceptance, particularly in primary care, physician groups are increasingly focusing on overall population health management use cases within the value-based care domain.

In terms of AI adoption, some domains are more mature than others. Those further along reflect the impact of market forces on physician group economics and the transition to value-based arrangements. For example, the clinical operations domain is more mature, given how central it is to a physician group's economics, patient access, and patient and clinician experience. In contrast, continuity of care, an important aspect of care management, is less mature given the fragmented nature of data across providers. However, new interoperability application programming interfaces (APIs), which enable the exchange of data between two organizations—such as two providers or a payer and a provider—are making it easier to exchange data in standard formats.

As with hospitals, five of the domains have a greater impact on administrative costs than on medical costs: continuity of care, network and market insights, value-based care, reimbursement, and corporate functions. These five domains are generally further along the adoption curve but likely have smaller total impact. Further, AI-enabled use cases in these domains tend to address existing processes. Future adoption in these domains is tied to market trends—such as the growth of value-based arrangements mentioned above—and the increase in vendors who can serve physician groups.

2.3.2.2   Case Study in Value-Based Care

One large physician group was in a value-based arrangement for a single chronic disease and searching for innovative ways to manage the total cost

Fig. 2.3 Physician group AI domains and example use cases

Domain	Description	Examples of AI-enabled use cases	Potential impact on total mission value[1]	Position on technology adoption curve[2]	Cost category affected[3]		Process type affected	
			Low / Med / High		Admin	Medical	Existing	New
Continuity of care	Optimizing point-of-service and referrals to improve patient care	Referral management, Patient transfers	High	D P S M	Admin		Existing	
Network and market insights	Tracking relationship strength among providers	Acute and post-acute provider segmentation, Benchmarking (e.g., quality, cost effectiveness)	Med	D P S M	Admin		Existing	
Clinical operations	Optimizing clinical workflow and practice operations	Operations (e.g., practice flow), Care team optimization, Supply chain optimization	High	D P S M		Medical	Existing	
Clinical analytics	Improving patient care journey with data at all points of care delivery	Clinical decision support, Treatment recommendations, Care pathway design	Med	D P S M		Medical		New
Quality and safety	Reducing adverse events with special attention to patient experience and legal compliance	Readmissions, Gap closure, Regulatory compliance	Med	D P S M		Medical		New
Value-based care	Improving patient outcomes with value-based care models	Patient stratification and risk scoring, Utilization management	Med	D P S M		Medical		New
Reimbursement	Automating and optimizing payment flows between providers and payers	Coding, Denials management	Low	D P S M	Admin		Existing	
Corporate functions	Managing back-office, administrative functions	Finance, Talent management		D P S M	Admin			New
Consumer	Understanding how best to engage consumers using tools	Segmentation and channel preference, Personalized engagement	Not included in sizing given use cases often are a net-zero activity across entities					

1. We define "total mission value" as the combination of financial and nonfinancial factors, such as quality outcomes, patient safety, patient experience, clinician satisfaction, and access to care.

2. D = development of solutions; P = piloting; S = scaling and adapting; M = mature.

3. Positioning represents the direct cost category affected; second-order effects may also reduce costs, but are not estimated.

Source: Authors' analysis

of care while improving outcomes for its patients. To meet those goals, the organization identified reducing preventable complications as an opportunity area. The organization observed that about 10 percent of patients were admitted to the hospital on a monthly basis. Using AI, the physician group developed a risk model to assess likelihood of unplanned admission. The AI application ingested data from several sources (for example, electronic health records, lab results, demographics, risk scores, and health information exchange admission, discharge, and transfer feeds) to develop the model and understand the main variables influencing unplanned admission. The initial model showed a potential decrease of several percentage points in inpatient spending due to better care management. The physician group is now planning to deploy the algorithm more broadly based on the prototype models. As a result, members of the care team will be able to better prioritize their outreach to patients, more efficiently using their time to improve patient outcomes. To operationalize this, the physician group is creating new clinical workflows that are helping the care team better focus their attention and resources.

2.3.3   Private Payers

2.3.3.1   Domain Breakdown

In our experience, AI-enabled use cases are emerging in six domains for private payers: health care management, provider relationship management, claims management, member services, corporate functions, and marketing and sales (figure 2.4).[4] Within health care management, private payers are focusing on care management, medical and clinical utilization and spending, and quality AI-enabled use cases. For example, private payers are attempting to predict behavioral health needs to better match patients with support resources and seeking to improve care management programs that help prevent avoidable readmissions. Another example is claims management, where private payers are using AI to improve auto-adjudication rates; predict and improve prior authorization outcomes to enable greater access to care; and prevent fraud, waste, and abuse. Further, the provider relationship management domain focuses on designing networks that enable better quality outcomes and access in a cost-effective way for members.

Adoption of AI varies across these domains. Claims management and corporate functions generally are more mature in their adoption of AI. Many use cases, such as processing a prior authorization or adjudicating a claim, are largely repetitive processes that are best suited for AI.

Three domains have more impact on administrative costs than on medi-

---

4. The marketing and sales domain is not included in our estimates because AI-enabled use cases in this domain often lead to a zero-sum outcome between private payers. Revenue for one organization is generally taken from another organization.

Fig. 2.4 Private payer AI domains and example use cases

Domain	Description	Examples of AI-enabled use cases	Potential impact on total mission value[1]			Position on technology adoption curve[2]	Cost category affected[3]		Process type affected	
			Low	Med	High		Admin	Medical	Existing	New
Healthcare management	Enhancing clinical and operational support to improve health outcomes	• Care management • Quality improvement • Medical and clinical utilization • Vendor management and optimization • Contact and outreach optimization			▬	D P			▲	
Provider relationship management	Optimizing provider relationships to decrease spending and improve outcomes for members	• Network design • Provider engagement • Value-based program management			▬	D P		▲	▲	
Claims management	Optimizing processes before, during, and after a claim is submitted	• Prior authorizations • Claims auto-adjudication • Fraud, waste, and abuse		▬		D S M	▲		▲	
Member services	Enhancing member and employer interactions with the organization	• Call center • Enrollment and billing		▬		D P S	▲		▲	
Corporate functions	Managing back-office, administrative functions	• Finance • Talent management	▬			D S	▲		▲	
Marketing and sales	Improving growth and product design	• Segmentation • Product design and pricing	*Not included in sizing given use cases often are a net-zero activity across entries*							

1. We define "total mission value" as the combination of financial and nonfinancial factors, such as quality outcomes, patient safety, patient experience, clinician satisfaction, and access to care.

2. D = development of solutions; P = piloting; S = scaling and adapting; M = mature.

3. Positioning represents the direct cost category affected; second-order effects may also reduce costs, but are not estimated.

Source: Authors' analysis

cal costs: claims management, member services, and corporate functions. The opportunity in these domains is substantial but less than for medical costs, given that administrative costs are a smaller portion of total costs. For the domains that are focused on medical cost, there are also large non-financial opportunities, including improving health, quality, and member experience. In general, use cases tend to be focused on existing processes across all domains.

2.3.3.2   Case Study in Claims Management

One large private payer, experiencing high costs and conducting an overall effort to improve its financial position, assessed areas for improvement in claims management. The analysis concluded that the organization could replace existing manual processes with AI to address fraud, waste, and abuse (FWA) among providers. As a result, a team built an AI classification model to identify potential FWA based on prior patterns observed in several years of claims data. The output of the model was a list of providers for further investigation. The team could then manually validate the list and determine next steps. This AI-enabled identification model allowed the payer to streamline operations and inform efforts that resulted in the reduction of medical costs by about 50 basis points. The payer's FWA team maintains the AI model on an ongoing basis.

2.3.3.3   Case Study in Health Care Management

To improve patient outcomes, a private payer focused on how to reduce the readmissions rate for its most vulnerable members. To address these readmissions, the organization developed an ML model that ingested a variety of claims and member demographic information. The output identified which patients were most likely to have a readmission, quantified the differences between these patients and those who did not have a readmission, and identified which parts of the care journey were linked to the readmission. The private payer then used the output to inform core business processes such as care management outreach. For example, the organization created a specialized outreach team of care managers who used the output to prioritize tactics for these vulnerable patients. As a result of this ML model and associated personalized marketing techniques, about 70 percent more members connected with their care managers compared with previous efforts that did not use the model. Follow-up visits with primary care physicians within 30 days of discharge increased by about 40 percent, and the all-cause readmission rate decreased by about 55 percent for this cohort.

2.4   Opportunity Size

Based on the domains discussed above, we have estimated the annual net savings that AI could create for US health care in the next five years.

Net savings is defined as total gross savings less annual expenses to operate AI. We derive the savings estimates for each domain from our experience working with health care organizations; there are few experimental studies of the impact of AI on costs or outcomes to inform our analysis. All savings estimates are based on the use of technologies available today and assume that adoption reaches full scale.

To estimate the total AI opportunity, we first estimate the revenue for each stakeholder group from 2019 National Health Expenditure data. Using McKinsey's proprietary value pool data, we subtract each stakeholder group's total earnings before interest and taxes (EBIT), leaving total costs. For hospitals and physician groups, we estimate three cost categories: administrative costs, medical costs associated with labor (for example, clinicians), and nonlabor medical costs (for example, diagnostics and supplies). For private payers, we estimate two cost categories: administrative costs and medical costs.

With this baseline, each AI domain described in the previous section is then aligned to a cost category. Based on our experience, we estimate a gross savings percentage for each domain. We break down what portion of these savings will affect administrative or medical costs. One key adjustment is converting gross savings to net savings, which represents the expense needed to maintain AI. Based on our experience, we model labor and technology maintenance expenses for each stakeholder group. The total amount is then subtracted from gross savings to estimate a net savings range.

We then multiply these percentages by the dollar values in each cost category to estimate a net savings value for each domain. Summing the estimated savings for each domain results in the total net savings opportunity for a stakeholder group. Figure 2.5 shows an example of the quality and safety domain for hospitals. We begin with total hospital revenue as reported in

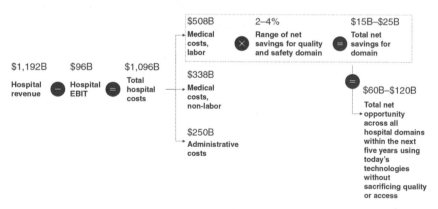

Fig. 2.5   Example of a hospital domain calculation: Quality and safety
Note: All data in 2019 dollars.
Source: National Health Expenditures data; authors' analysis

the National Health Expenditure data of $1,192 billion in 2019. We subtract hospital EBIT to estimate a total for hospital costs. Total hospital costs are then broken into three cost categories. The quality and safety domain largely affects labor within medical costs, which we estimate to be $508 billion in 2019. Using the net savings rate for this domain (after accounting for the gross-to-net conversion), total net savings is $15 billion to $25 billion. Repeating this for all the domains, we estimate a total annual net savings opportunity for hospitals of $60 billion to $120 billion within the next five years using today's technologies without sacrificing quality or access.

To consider the full AI opportunity in health care, we also include public payers and other sites of care such as dentists and home health. For public payers, we begin with the AI opportunity estimate for private payers, which have several similar functions and operations. Referencing previous research, we estimate the total costs to be about 45 percent of those for private payers (Sahni et al. 2021). We further assume the savings opportunity would be about three-quarters that of private payers given that public payers do not undertake all the same functions to the same extent, such as provider relationship management and health care management. For other sites of care, we begin with the AI opportunity estimate for physician groups. Similarly referencing previous research, we estimate the total costs to be about 115 percent of those for physician groups (Sahni et al. 2021). We further assume the savings opportunity would be about half that of physician groups given differences in patient acuity, clinical staff mix (for example, less clinician time per clinical episode), and fewer applicable AI domains.

Our estimates do not include one-time implementation costs, which in our experience are 1.0 to 1.5 times the annual net savings. One-time implementation costs relate directly to building an AI-enabled use case, which includes hiring specialized talent, creating incremental infrastructure or computing power, and aggregating and cleaning the necessary data. One-time implementation costs do not include large investments such as new underlying core technology or last-mile change management, both of which could be necessary and can vary greatly by organization.

2.4.1 Hospitals

In 2019 dollars, total costs for hospitals are about $1,096 billion, of which 80 percent is medical and 20 percent is administrative. With about 6,000 hospitals nationally, this is a fragmented market. The top 10 hospital systems accounted for about 18 percent of admissions in 2017 (Sahni et al. 2019). Types of facilities include community hospitals and academic medical centers. The typical hospital has an "all-payer margin" of about 6 to 7 percent (Medicare Payment Advisory Commission 2022).

Based on our calculations, hospitals employing AI-enabled use cases could achieve total annual run-rate net savings of $60 billion to $120 billion (roughly 4 to 10 percent of total costs for hospitals) within the next five years using today's technologies without sacrificing quality or access. Clinical operations—encompassing emergency room and inpatient care, capacity and workflow, diagnostics, supply chain, and clinical workforce management—and quality and safety are the primary drivers of this opportunity. About 40 percent of total savings would come from reducing administrative costs (roughly 9 to 19 percent of this cost category), with the remaining 60 percent from reducing medical costs (roughly 4 to 8 percent of this cost category). About 45 percent of total savings would come from simplifying existing processes, with the remaining 55 percent from creating new processes.

2.4.2 Physician Groups

In 2019 dollars, total costs for physician groups are about $711 billion, of which 70 percent is medical and 30 percent administrative. The physician group landscape is fragmented, with about 125,000 groups nationally, including those employed by hospitals, owned by private organizations, or independent (Sahni et al. 2021).

Based on our calculations, physician groups employing AI-enabled use cases could achieve total annual run-rate net savings of $20 billion to $60 billion (roughly 3 to 8 percent of total costs for physician groups) within the next five years using today's technologies without sacrificing quality or access. The main domain of opportunity, similar to hospitals, is clinical operations, with a focus on outpatient operations and access, supply chain, and clinical workforce management. About 50 percent of total savings would come from reducing administrative costs (roughly 4 to 14 percent of this cost category), with the remaining 50 percent from reducing medical costs (roughly 2 to 6 percent of this cost category). About 45 percent of total savings would come from simplifying existing processes, with the remaining 55 percent from creating new processes.

2.4.3 Private Payers

In 2019 dollars, total costs for private payers are about $1,135 billion, of which 85 percent is medical and 15 percent administrative. In 2017, the top five private payers plus Medicare (Part A/B only) and Medicaid (fee-for-service only) accounted for about 58 percent of covered lives, and the 350-plus other private payers covered the remaining 42 percent (Sahni et al. 2019). Types of private payers include national, regional, and local for-profit and not-for-profit organizations.

Based on our calculations, private payers could achieve total annual run-rate net savings of $80 billion to $110 billion (roughly 7 to 9 percent of total costs for private payers) within the next five years using today's technologies without sacrificing quality or access. The primary domains of opportunity are health care management (including care management and avoidable readmissions), claims management (including FWA identification, prior authorizations, and adjudication), and provider relationship management (including network design, value-based care, and provider directory management). About 20 percent of total savings would come from reducing administrative costs (roughly 8 to 14 percent of this cost category), with the remaining 80 percent from reducing medical costs (roughly 6 to 9 percent of this cost category). About 55 percent of total savings would come from simplifying existing processes, with the remaining 45 percent from creating new processes.

2.4.4   Overall

With these estimates, we then scale the savings to the entire US health care industry (table 2.1). In 2019 dollars, we estimate the annual run-rate net savings to be $200 billion to $360 billion within the next five years using today's technologies without sacrificing quality or access. This would amount to a 5 to 10 percent overall reduction in US health care spending. AI adoption could also create nonfinancial benefits such as improved health care quality, increased access, better patient experience, and greater clinician satisfaction. (In this paper, we do not offer an estimate of these nonfinancial benefits.)

Administrative costs could be reduced by 7 to 14 percent, roughly $65 billion to $135 billion annually. This is about 35 percent of total savings. The remaining 65 percent could reduce medical costs by 5 to 8 percent, roughly $130 billion to $235 billion annually. The overall AI opportunity is divided nearly equally between simplifying existing processes and creating new processes.

2.5   Adoption Challenges

Despite the large opportunity, the AI adoption rate in health care has lagged behind that in other industries (Cam, Chui, and Hall 2019). Generally, technology adoption follows an S-curve—first developing solutions, then piloting, followed by scaling and adapting, and finally reaching maturity. Other industries have already reached the final stage of the S-curve; for example, financial services companies deploy sophisticated AI algorithms for fraud detection, credit assessments, and customer acquisition. Mining companies use AI to boost output, reduce costs, and manage the environmental impact of new projects. Retailers use AI to predict which goods will interest a customer based on the customer's shopping history.

Across nearly all the domains identified in section 2.2, AI adoption in health care is at an earlier stage of the S-curve. There are several possible reasons for this. Many economists believe that AI is underused because the health care payment system does not provide incentives for this type of innovation. Another view is that management barriers, both at the organizational and industry level, are responsible for slower adoption in health care.

Table 2.1   Breakdown of overall AI net savings opportunity within next five years using today's technology without sacrificing quality or access

Stakeholder group	Total costs (2019), $ billions	Net savings opportunity (2019), $ billions	Net savings opportunity as percent of stakeholder group's total costs	Percentage of net savings opportunity focused on administrative costs
Hospitals	$1,096	$60–$120	5–11%	~40%
Physician groups	$711	$20–$60	3–8%	~50%
Private payers	$1,135	$80–$110	7–10%	~20%
Public payers	$511	$30–$40	5–7%	~20%
Other sites of care	$817	$10–$30	1–4%	~50%
Total		**$200–$360**	**5–10%**[a]	**~35%**

Source: National Health Expenditures data; authors' analysis.

[a] This represents the percent of total national health spending in 2019.

In this paper, we do not settle the debate about whether better incentives will lead to greater adoption of AI. Rather, we discuss the managerial difficulties in bringing AI to bear in health care. Even if the right payment models were in place, organizations would still need to overcome challenges such as legacy technology, siloed data, nascent operating models, misaligned incentives, industry fragmentation, and talent attraction (Goldfarb and Teodoridis 2022; Henke et al. 2016).

In our experience, private payers are further along the AI adoption curve than other health care organizations, although larger national private payers with greater resources are more advanced in their use of AI compared with smaller regional private payers that may face resource and talent attraction challenges. Hospitals have piloted AI and are beginning to scale adoption in some domains, with larger hospitals having done more than smaller hospitals. Most physician groups are at the beginning of their journey (unless employed by hospitals).

In this section, we discuss specifics about what is needed for AI adoption in health care. We break these down into "within" and "between/seismic" factors. "Within" factors are those that can be controlled and implemented by individual organizations. "Between" factors require collaboration between organizations but not broader, industry-wide change, and "seismic" factors require broad, structural collaboration across the US health care industry (Sahni et al. 2021).

2.5.1 "Within" Challenges

In our experience, successful AI adoption depends on six factors (figure 2.6). These are the same for all organizations across industries, though some of the underlying challenges are specific to health care.

The first factor is a **mission-led roadmap**. The roadmap should offer a clear view of value, link to business objectives and mission, and be sequenced for implementation. A key challenge is ensuring the end state is a transformative view of the organization, not incremental. Each AI-enabled use case should be quantified, which presents additional hurdles for health care organizations because value extends into nonfinancial factors such as quality outcomes, patient safety, patient experience, clinician satisfaction, and access to care. As noted above, we refer to this combination of financial and nonfinancial factors as total mission value. In our experience, the most successful organizations rely on strong collaboration between business and technology leaders to develop and implement this roadmap.

A second factor is **talent**. Organizations must ensure that the right skills and capabilities are available across the organization. Talent shortages are common, especially in AI (Zwetsloot, Heston, and Arnold 2019). Many organizations have addressed these shortages by establishing talent hubs, sometimes in a different city with operations than headquarters, but many health care organizations face the additional challenge of being inherently

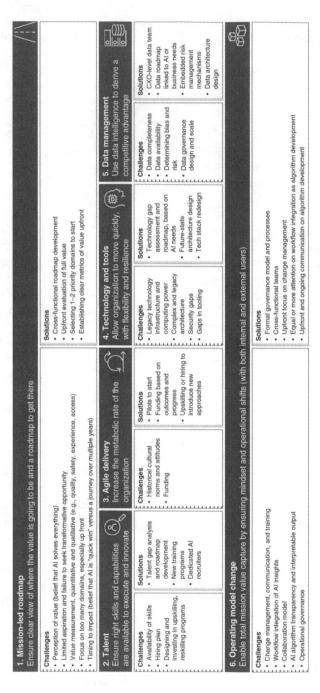

1. Mission-led roadmap
Ensure clear view of where the value is going to be and a roadmap to get there

Challenges
- Perception of value (belief that AI solves everything)
- Limited aspiration and failure to seek transformative opportunity
- Value measurement, quantitative and qualitative (e.g., quality, safety, experience, access)
- Focus on too many domains, especially up front
- Timing to impact (belief that AI is "quick win" versus a journey over multiple years)

Solutions
- Cross-functional roadmap development
- Upfront evaluation of full value
- Selecting 1–2 priority domains to start
- Establishing clear metrics of value upfront

2. Talent
Ensure right skills and capabilities are available to execute and innovate

Challenges
- Availability of skills
- Hiring plan
- Designing and investing in upskilling, reskilling programs

Solutions
- Talent gap analysis and roadmap development
- New training programs
- Dedicated AI recruiters

3. Agile delivery
Increase the metabolic rate of the organization

Challenges
- Historical cultural norms and attitudes
- Funding

Solutions
- Pilots to start
- Funding based on outcomes and progress
- Upskilling or hiring to introduce new approaches

4. Technology and tools
Allow organization to move quickly, with flexibility and resilience

Challenges
- Legacy technology infrastructure and computing power
- Complex and legacy architecture
- Security gaps
- Gaps in tooling

Solutions
- Technology gap assessment and roadmap, based on AI needs
- Future-state architecture design
- Tech stack redesign

5. Data management
Use data intelligence to derive a competitive advantage

Challenges
- Data completeness
- Data availability
- Determining bias and risk
- Data governance design and scale

Solutions
- CXO-level data team
- Data roadmap linked to AI or business needs
- Embedded risk management mechanisms
- Data architecture design

6. Operating model change
Enable total mission value capture by ensuring mindset and operational shifts (with both internal and external users)

Challenges
- Change management, communication, and training
- Workflow integration of AI insights
- Collaboration model
- AI algorithm transparency and interpretable output
- Operational governance

Solutions
- Formal governance model and processes
- Cross-functional teams
- Upfront focus on change management
- Equal or more attention on workflow integration as algorithm development
- Upfront and ongoing communication on algorithm development

Fig. 2.6 **Factors for successful AI adoption with associated challenges and solutions within health care organizations**

Source: Carey et al. (2021); Rajkomar et al. (2019); Bates et al. (2020); Shaw et al. (2019); Singh et al. (2020); He et al. (2019); Authors' analysis.

local. Still, some are experimenting with ways to make this work—for example, by centralizing talent in a nearby location or using remote work options.

Agile delivery, or accelerating an organization's decision-making and delivery processes, is a new approach for many health care organizations. Changing the culture to move away from historical processes and ways of working is a challenge for organizations in all industries. It is an especially large hurdle in health care, where culture is often more deeply rooted than in other industries, and where clinicians are justifiably concerned that the process of change might harm patients. In our experience, organizations that empower small, integrated agile teams are more likely to have successful AI deployments.

Enabling agile delivery requires **technology and tools** that are flexible, scalable, secure, and resilient. Organizations in all industries confront complex legacy IT environments. This is particularly true in health care given the relatively low levels of investment in technology and high levels of customization. In our experience, successful deployments generally overinvest in the enablers of AI, such as core technology architecture and data systems.

Data management, or the use of data to derive a competitive advantage, is often overlooked in AI deployments, though it is one of the most critical factors. Organizations in all industries face key challenges with data fragmentation and quality. The challenge is even greater in health care given the large number of systems, general lack of interoperability, and data privacy and usage requirements. In our experience, the most successful AI deployments establish a dedicated function to manage all data at the beginning of any adoption journey.

Finally, establishing the right **operating model** is key.[5] Such a model enables an organization to capture full mission value by encouraging mindset and operational shifts among both internal and external users. Determining the right operating model is difficult in any industry, and the number of stakeholders, need for change management with providers, and heightened attention to security and model risk increase the challenge in health care. In our experience, organizations that deploy more central structures to build capabilities, consistency, and rigor from the beginning position themselves for more successful AI deployments, while setting up the operating model to work closely with their business partners.

While it is critical for organizations to pursue all six factors, it is just as important to foster "digital trust" among individuals—to inspire confidence that the organization effectively protects data, uses AI responsibly, and provides transparency. Building this trust requires organizations to establish the right controls, processes, and risk management. Without digital trust and

---

5. *Operating model* encompasses a number of components about an organization, including structure, governance, and processes.

the responsible use of AI, health care organizations may experience greater scrutiny and a slower pace of use-case scaling.

Investing in addressing these challenges is critical. Across industries, the highest performers spent 30 to 60 percent more than others when adopting technologies such as AI and expect to increase their budgets 10 to 15 percent over the following year. Meanwhile, lesser performers report small or no increases (D'Silva and Lawler 2022).

2.5.2   "Between" and "Seismic" Challenges

Even if a health care organization successfully deploys AI, it will face ongoing industry-level challenges—factors that are out of the organization's control and can hinder widespread adoption. These include data heterogeneity, lack of patient confidence, ongoing adaptability, the ability to capture productivity gains, and regulatory challenges (figure 2.7).

These industry-level challenges take two forms: social and technology. By *social challenge* we mean one in which the industry would need to encourage stakeholders such as physicians to adopt the same approach, process, or standard. By *technology challenge* we mean one in which the hurdle to adoption relates to the need for a technology solution.

Data heterogeneity in health care takes many forms. In industries with greater AI adoption, most data are structured. In health care, by contrast, large portions of key data are unstructured, existing in electronic health records. Clinical notes, the clinician's recording of a patient's response to a particular treatment, are one example. Further, these data exist in multiple sources, often with limited ways to connect disparate pieces of information for an individual patient (Kruse et al. 2016).

Challenge	Description	Types of challenge[1]	
		Social	Technology
Data heterogeneity	Large portions of needed healthcare data are unstructured, spread across multiple data sources, and stored in varying data structures		✓
Lack of patient confidence	Patients lack confidence in output due to concerns about the privacy of their data, potential biases in data affecting AI outputs, uncertainty about methodology, and clarity of the reports	✓	
Ongoing adaptability	Once launched, AI models may be slow to adapt or integrate new data when released		✓
Ability to capture productivity gains	Once AI frees up capacity of clinicians or assets such as operating rooms, it may not be applied to increase productivity	✓	
Regulatory challenges	Evolving regulations that could increase adoption may require approval processes for validation for organizations such as CMS or FDA	✓	✓

Fig. 2.7   Industry-level challenges by type

1. By *social challenge*, we mean one in which the industry would need to encourage stakeholders such as physicians to adopt the same approach, process, or standard. By *technology challenge*, we mean one in which the hurdle to adoption relates to the need for a technology solution.

Source: Authors' analysis

Patient confidence in AI output is also critical to the integration of information into the clinical workflow. One issue is privacy. Patients may worry about how their data are being used and prevent the application of AI for their medical needs. Another concern is whether AI output can be trusted. There are many examples of biases in algorithms, and patients may not trust AI-generated information even if a clinician validates it. There are also methodological concerns such as validation and communication of uncertainty, as well as reporting difficulties such as explanations of assumptions (Bates et al. 2020; Shaw et al. 2019; Singh et al. 2020; He et al. 2019).

In addition, questions arise about whether AI-enabled use cases would cement certain biases in existing data and be slow to respond to new types of data. For example, an organization using AI to help define clinical treatment pathways might need to control for biases in existing treatment recommendations and determine how to remove them. In addition to adding AI ethics to model development, organizations are addressing bias by creating synthetic data—manufactured data designed to train a model on a certain set of inputs, similar to real-world data. Further, as health care generates new data, these changes may require previously developed models to be refreshed.

Many clinicians and health care executives are optimistic that AI could address ongoing productivity challenges in health care. Historical analyses have shown negative labor productivity growth in health care and a likelihood that clinician shortages will continue (Sahni et al. 2019; Berlin et al. 2022). If adopted appropriately, AI could free up clinician capacity. The question arises, though, whether clinicians will use the excess capacity to see more patients or to complete nonclinical tasks.

Finally, in the United States, regulations generally focus on protecting the patient, given the private and sensitive nature of each person's data. But regulation also plays other roles in AI. For example, Medicare and Medicaid are beginning to reimburse for AI applications, though adoption is still in the early stages. This is unique to health care; organizations in other industries have to pay for AI themselves. Validation that algorithms are clinically robust and safe is another issue. For example, the Food and Drug Administration established standards for evaluating software as a medical device and AI-enabled medical devices. Dozens of AI products have since received approval, the majority in the past five years. Examples of digitally enabled therapeutics include those for treating type 2 diabetes and substance use disorder. This type of industry-level change could provide greater confidence for patients and clinicians using AI.

2.6   Changes That May Improve AI Adoption

Based on our experience, fewer than 10 percent of health care organizations today fully integrate AI technologies into their business processes. But the benefits of doing so are meaningful: in our experience, organizations that deploy AI have twice the five-year revenue compound annual growth rate compared with others that do not. With a $200 billion to $360 billion opportunity in health care and such a small subset of organizations capturing the potential, what might the future hold? Will AI adoption accelerate?

Several trends suggest the tide may soon turn. First, the COVID-19 pandemic, coupled with rising inflation and labor shortages, is straining the finances of health care organizations (Singhal and Patel 2022). For example, all seven of the largest publicly traded payers have announced productivity improvement programs in the past few years. Further, research shows that the most successful organizations coming out of a recession generally have run larger productivity improvement programs (Görner et al. 2022). This could be a boon for the adoption of AI-enabled use cases—especially use cases that focus on administrative costs, which are usually passed over in favor of a focus on medical costs.

A second trend is the flow of investment into AI technologies, even in today's uncertain macroeconomic climate. From 2014 to 2021, the overall number of venture capital–backed health care AI start-ups increased more than fivefold. Over the same period, the number of private equity deals for health care AI organizations increased more than threefold.

At the organizational level, there are indications that the C-suite's appreciation for the potential of technologies like AI is growing. For example, nearly all of the top 15 private payers have a designated chief analytics or chief data officer. Dozens of hospitals do as well, including most of the largest in the United States. This elevation of business importance suggests that more AI deployments may be on the way.

At the industry level, evolving regulations may enable the creation of new data sets that feed AI. For example, recently introduced medical price transparency regulations promise to increase the availability of hospital and private payer data. Alone, these data may not be good enough for AI algorithms to generate insights; however, if coupled with other data sets, such as member or census data, they could accelerate the adoption of AI. In addition, the Centers for Medicare and Medicaid Services has been developing interoperability rules and APIs that require data to be made available in a consistent structure to be exchanged across organizations.

2.7   Conclusions

The promise of AI in health care has been a topic of discussion in the industry for more than a decade. But its potential has not been quantified systematically, and adoption has been lacking. We estimate that AI in health care offers a $200 billion to $360 billion annual run-rate net savings opportunity that can be achieved within the next five years using today's technologies without sacrificing quality or access. These opportunities could also result in nonfinancial benefits such as improved health care quality, increased access, better patient experience, and greater clinician satisfaction. As our case studies highlight, both the challenges to adoption and actionable solutions are becoming better understood as more organizations pilot AI. Recent market trends also suggest that AI in health care may be at a tipping point.

Still, taking full advantage of the savings opportunity will require the deployment of many AI-enabled use cases across multiple domains. Ongoing research and validation of these use cases is needed. This could include conducting randomized control trials to prove the impact of AI in clinical domains to increase confidence for broader deployment. However, given that these studies will likely require a long timeline, additional work focused on case studies of successful deployments may provide greater evidence for organizations to overcome internal inertia in the near term. Finally, an independent third party could create a central data repository of AI deployments—both successful and unsuccessful—which would allow for more robust econometric analyses to inform rapid scaling.

As other industries have shown, AI as a technology could have an outsized financial and nonfinancial impact in health care, enabling patients to receive better care at a lower cost. The next few years will determine whether this promise becomes a reality.

References

Allen, B., S. Agarwal, L. Coombs, C. Wald, and K. Dreyer. 2021. "2020 ACR Data Science Institute Artificial Intelligence Survey." *Journal of the American College of Radiology* 18 (8): 1153–59.

Bates, D. W., A. Auerbach, P. Schulam, A. Wright, and S. Saria. 2020. "Reporting and Implementing Interventions Involving Machine Learning and Artificial Intelligence." *Annals of Internal Medicine* 172 (11 Suppl): S137–S144.

Bates, D. W., D. Levine, A. Syrowatka, M. Kuznetsova, K. J. T. Craig, A. Rui, G. Purcell Jackson, and K. Rhee. 2021. "The Potential of Artificial Intelligence to Improve Patient Safety: A Scoping Review." *NPJ Digital Medicine* 4 (1): 54.

Berlin, G., M. LaPointe, M. Murphy, and J. Wexler. 2022. "Assessing the Lingering Impact of COVID-19 on the Nursing Workforce." McKinsey & Company, May 11, 2022. https://www.mckinsey.com/industries/healthcare/our-insights/assessing-the-lingering-impact-of-covid-19-on-the-nursing-workforce.

Berwick, D. M., and A. D. Hackbarth. 2012. "Eliminating Waste in US Health Care." *Journal of the American Medical Association* 307 (14): 1513–16.

Cam, A., M. Chui, and B. Hall. 2019. "Global AI Survey: AI Proves Its Worth, but Few Scale Impact." McKinsey & Company, November 22, 2019. https://www.mckinsey.com/featured-insights/artificial-intelligence/global-ai-survey-ai-proves-its-worth-but-few-scale-impact.

Carey, D., R. Charan, E. Lamarre, K. Smaje, and R. Zemmel. 2021. "The CEO's Playbook for a Successful Digital Transformation." *Harvard Business Review*, December 20, 2021.

Cooley-Rieders, K., and K. Zheng. 2021. "Physician Documentation Matters. Using Natural Language Processing to Predict Mortality in Sepsis." *Intelligence-Based Medicine* 5: 100028.

D'Silva, V., and B. Lawler. 2022. "What Makes a Company Successful at Using AI?" *Harvard Business Review*, February 28, 2022.

Goldfarb, A., and F. Teodoridis. 2022. "Why Is AI Adoption in Health Care Lagging?" *Brookings*, March 9, 2022. https://www.brookings.edu/articles/why-is-ai-adoption -in-health-care-lagging/.

Görner, S., A. Govindarajan, A. Panas, E. Greenberg, A. Kelkar, J. Kelleher, I. Kristensen, L. Liu, A. Padhi, and Z. Silverman. 2022. "Something's Coming: How US Companies Can Build Resilience, Survive a Downturn, and Thrive in the Next Cycle." McKinsey & Company, September 16, 2022. https://www.mckinsey .com/capabilities/risk-and-resilience/our-insights/somethings-coming-how-us -companies-can-build-resilience-survive-a-downturn-and-thrive-in-the-next -cycle

He, J., S. L. Baxter, J. Xu, J. Xu, X. Zhou, and K. Zhang. 2019. "The Practical Implementation of Artificial Intelligence Technologies in Medicine." *Nature Medicine* 25 (1): 30–36.

Henke, N., J. Bughin, M. Chui, J. Manyika, T. Saleh, B. Wiseman, and G. Sethupathy. 2016. "The Age of Analytics: Competing in a Data-Driven World." McKinsey & Company, December 7, 2016. https://www.mckinsey.com/capabilities /quantumblack/our-insights/the-age-of-analytics-competing-in-a-data-driven -world

Kilic, A., A. Goyal, J. K. Miller, E. Gjekmarkaj, W. L. Tam, T. G. Gleason, I. Sultan, and A. Dubrawksi. 2020. "Predictive Utility of a Machine Learning Algorithm in Estimating Mortality Risk in Cardiac Surgery." *Annals of Thoracic Surgery* 109 (6): 1811–19.

Kruse, C. S., R. Goswamy, Y. Raval, and S. Marawi. 2016. "Challenges and Opportunities of Big Data in Health Care: A Systematic Review." *JMIR Medical Informatics* 4 (4): e38.

Luo, L., F. Zhang, Y. Yao, R. Gong, M. Fu, and J. Xiao. 2020. "Machine Learning for Identification of Surgeries with High Risks of Cancellation." *Health Informatics Journal* 26 (1): 141–55.

Medicare Payment Advisory Commission. 2022. *March 2022 Report to the Congress: Medicare Payment Policy*. March 15, 2022. https://www.medpac.gov/wp-content /uploads/2022/03/Mar22_MedPAC_ReportToCongress_v3_SEC.pdf.

Nemati, S., A. Holder, F. Razmi, M. D. Stanley, G. D. Clifford, and T. G. Buchman. 2018. "An Interpretable Machine Learning Model for Accurate Prediction of Sepsis in the ICU." *Critical Care Medicine* 46 (4): 547–53.

Rajkomar, A., J. Dean, and I. Kohane. 2019. "Machine Learning in Medicine." *New England Journal of Medicine* 380 (14): 1347–58.

Sahni, N. R., P. Kumar, E. Levine, and S. Singhal. 2019. "The Productivity Imperative for Healthcare Delivery in the United States." McKinsey & Company, February 27, 2019. https://www.mckinsey.com/industries/healthcare/our-insights/the -productivity-imperative-for-healthcare-delivery-in-the-united-states.

Sahni, N. R., P. Mishra, B. Carrus, and D. M. Cutler. 2021. "Administrative Simplification: How to Save a Quarter-Trillion Dollars in US Healthcare." McKinsey & Company, October 20, 2021. https://www.mckinsey.com/industries/healthcare

/our-insights/administrative-simplification-how-to-save-a-quarter-trillion-dollars
-in-us-healthcare.

Shaw, J., F. Rudzicz, T. Jamieson, and A. Goldfarb. 2019. "Artificial Intelligence
and the Implementation Challenge." *Journal of Medical Internet Research* 21 (7):
e13659.

Singh, R. P., G. L. Hom, M. D. Abramoff, J. P. Campbell, and M. F. Chiang. 2020.
"Current Challenges and Barriers to Real-World Artificial Intelligence Adoption
for the Healthcare System, Provider, and the Patient." *Translational Vision Science
& Technology* 9 (2): 45.

Singhal, S., and N. Patel. 2022. "The Future of US Healthcare: What's Next for the
Industry Post-COVID-19." McKinsey & Company, July 19, 2022. https://www
.mckinsey.com/industries/healthcare/our-insights/the-future-of-us-healthcare
-whats-next-for-the-industry-post-covid-19.

Society of Automotive Engineers. 2021. *Taxonomy and Definitions for Terms Related
to Driving Automation Systems for On-Road Motor Vehicles.* https://www.sae.org
/standards/content/j3016_202104/.

Zwetsloot, R., R. Heston, and Z. Arnold. 2019. *Strengthening the U.S. AI Workforce:
A Policy and Research Agenda.* Georgetown Center for Security and Emerging
Technology. September 2019. https://cset.georgetown.edu/wp-content/uploads
/CSET_US_AI_Workforce.pdf.

Comment   David C. Chan Jr.

In their very interesting piece, Sahni et al. estimate the potential impact of
artificial intelligence (AI) on healthcare spending. As the authors note, AI
has the potential to create more efficient processes and to improve decision
making. These potential impacts could lead to productivity improvements,
reducing the costs of delivering healthcare while improving outcomes.

The authors bring a unique mix of experience and perspectives from
management consulting and economics. Collectively, they draw on industry
knowledge and hands-on experience interacting with healthcare institutions
seeking to implement AI to improve their processes. With this background,
they conduct a costing analysis, breaking down the healthcare industry into
five "stakeholder groups": hospitals, physician groups, private payers, public
payers, and other sites of care (e.g., dental and home health care). Within
each of these stakeholder groups, they further analyze nine domains—
continuity of care, network and market insights, clinical operations, clinical
analytics, quality and safety, value-based care, reimbursement, corporate

David C. Chan Jr. is an associate professor of health policy at Stanford University and a
research associate of the National Bureau of Economic Research.

For acknowledgments, sources of research support, and disclosure of the author's material financial relationships, if any, please see https://www.nber.org/books-and-chapters
/economics-artificial-intelligence-health-care-challenges/comment-potential-impact
-artificial-intelligence-healthcare-spending-jr.

functions, and consumer—for hospitals and physician groups each and six domains for private payers—healthcare management, provider relationship management, claims management, member services, corporate functions, and marketing and sales.

As the authors state, they mostly draw on insights and experience without relying on experimental or quasi-experimental evidence that most economists would be more familiar with. Based on their analysis, they conclude that AI could lead to 5 to 10 percent lower US healthcare spending, about $200 billion to $360 billion annually in 2019 dollars, within five years and without reducing quality or access. Nonetheless, they note that AI adoption has lagged in the healthcare industry relative to other industries. To explain the lack of adoption, they focus on "managerial challenges," including "legacy technology, siloed data, nascent operating models, misaligned incentives, industry fragmentation, and talent attraction." They note market trends that suggest a mitigation of these challenges and an acceleration in the pace of AI adoption.

As a physician and health economist, the first question I have is the following: What makes technology adoption different in healthcare relative to other industries? Since Arrow (1963) and continuing with Cutler (2010), health economists have produced insights into differences in healthcare relative to other industries and the implications of these differences for productivity. Given the fee-for-service payment system and the high degree of market concentration in the industry, improving efficiency by reducing costs has not typically been the way for healthcare delivery systems to increase profits. As we know from efforts at healthcare reform, change in the industry will need to be filtered through stakeholder groups with powerful informational or institutional advantages. New technologies such as AI will need to be adopted by these stakeholder groups; if adopted, they will naturally be used for the benefit of these groups. If it is not in the best interests of these groups to reduce costs, then cost reduction may not come to fruition even with highly effective technologies.

The managerial challenges that the paper casts are somewhat generic—there seems to be little insight into why "legacy technology" and "talent challenges" should be a bigger barrier in healthcare relative to other industries. Is there a reason why healthcare should have talent challenges relative to other industries? To explain why AI adoption or AI impact has lagged in healthcare relative to other industries, it seems crucial to link these phenomena to underlying economic differences between healthcare and other industries. It may be instructive to review the string of technological tools that have come before AI in the past. For example, health IT has previously been cast as a technology with the potential to reduce costs, saving patients from unnecessary utilization and adverse events. However, despite the availability of health IT systems, less than 5 percent of hospitals adopted a health IT by 2008, when they were heavily incentivized by federal legislation to adopt health IT products (Jha et al. 2008). Healthcare systems rarely integrated data with other systems, again until legislated to do so (Adler-Milstein et al. 2014). In my view, health IT provides one of many cautionary examples of economic incentives imbedded in institutions and policies shaping the use and the features of a new technology.

Sahni et al. present a useful step forward in envisioning the potential impact of AI on healthcare spending. As they note, they lack citations to existing experimental and quasi-experimental evidence to form the basis of their opinions. The lack of existing evidence is a fine justification for using expert opinion to weigh in on an important question. However, in future work, I would be eager to see the gap filled by a more data-driven approaches, even if the data are simply correlational. Heterogeneity in adoption and in effect is the rule in healthcare rather than the exception. A closer look at the characteristics of healthcare systems that have adopted AI and the effects of adoption on spending and outcomes would likely yield significant insights into the intended and unintended consequences of AI on the healthcare industry as a whole.

References

Adler-Milstein, Julia, Catherine M. DesRoches, Michael F. Furukawa, Chantal Worzala, Dustin Charles, Peter Kralovec, Samantha Stalley, and Ashish K. Jha. 2014. "More Than Half of US Hospitals Have at Least a Basic EHR, but Stage 2 Criteria Remain Challenging for Most." *Health Affairs* 33 (9): 1664–71.

Arrow, Kenneth J. 1963. "Uncertainty and the Welfare Economics of Medical Care." *American Economic Review* 53 (5): 941–73.

Cutler, David. 2010. "Where Are the Health Care Entrepreneurs?" *Issues in Science and Technology* 27 (1): 49–56.

Jha, Ashish K., Catherine M. DesRoches, Eric G. Campbell, Karen Donelan, Sowmya R. Rao, Timothy G. Ferris, Alexandra Shields, Sara Rosenbaum, and David Blumenthal. 2009. "Use of Electronic Health Records in U.S. Hospitals." *New England Journal of Medicine* 360 (16): 1628–38.

Comment   Mark Sendak, Freya Gulamali, and Suresh Balu

Introduction

While enthusiasm for the role of artificial intelligence (AI) in healthcare continues to mount, economic analyses demonstrating successful return on investment are scant. In their piece titled "The Potential Impact of Artificial Intelligence on Healthcare Administrative Spending," Sahni and colleagues estimate the total potential savings from AI in healthcare to be $200 billion to $360 billion annually. These estimates will likely spur further investment in the development and adoption of healthcare AI. However, unless stakeholders rapidly align on strategies to overcome barriers and achieve the required activation energy, the potential value of healthcare AI will remain beyond reach.

We represent the Duke Institute for Health Innovation (DIHI) at Duke Health, a multihospital health system with 67,000 inpatient admissions and 4.7 million outpatient visits annually (Duke Health 2023). Similar to Sahni and colleagues, we draw upon a combination of academic and industry experience. We have nearly a decade of experience working on internal innovation projects that design, develop, and integrate novel technologies and care delivery models within Duke Health. Through our work at DIHI, we have developed and implemented over 15 AI solutions internally and have multiple initiatives validating AI solutions in external health systems. We also launched the Health AI Partnership (HAIP) in 2021 to convene stakeholders from health systems across the United States to advance the ethical adoption of AI (Duke Institute for Health Innovation 2021). Through our work at HAIP, we have conducted 85 interviews with clinical, technical, and operational leaders across nearly a dozen health systems in the US to surface and disseminate AI adoption best practices. While we work across care delivery settings and medical conditions, our perspective is primarily grounded in the experience of health systems and physician practices.

In this comment, we present several analyses that complement the work of Sahni and colleagues. First, we describe concrete use cases that reinforce the hospital AI delivery domains and the need to capture both financial and nonfinancial benefits. Second, we present on-the-ground insights that identify gaps in evidence relied upon by Sahni and colleagues. Lastly, we

Mark Sendak is the population health & data science lead at the Duke Institute for Health Innovation.

Freya Gulamali is a research analyst at the Duke Institute for Health Innovation.

Suresh Balu is associate dean for innovation and partnership at the Duke University School of Medicine, and program director of the Duke Institute for Health Innovation.

For acknowledgments, sources of research support, and disclosure of the authors' material financial relationships, if any, please see https://www.nber.org/books-and-chapters/economics -artificial-intelligence-health-care-challenges/overcoming-activation-energy-required -unlock-value-ai-healthcare-sendak.

identify specific organizational (within-health-system) and seismic (policy-level) interventions that could overcome the activation energy to unlock the value of healthcare AI.

AI Delivery Domains

In this section, we present use cases from DIHI and HAIP that illustrate the AI delivery domains described by Sahni and colleagues. We focus on the six domains related to direct patient care and not related to reimbursement or corporate functions.

The first AI delivery domain is continuity of care, described as "optimizing point-of-service and referrals to improve patient care." Within this domain, our team at DIHI used AI to predict hospital readmissions to optimize postdischarge transfers to skilled nursing facilities (SNFs). Geriatric patients discharged to SNFs are at increased risk of hospital readmission, and AI can prioritize patients for telemedicine support to ensure appropriate postacute care (Krol et al. 2019; Bellantoni et al. 2022). This use of AI can create financial value in value-based care programs by preventing hospital readmissions and nonfinancial value by improving the safety and quality of care provided within SNFs.

Second, network and market insight applications are described as "tracking relationship strength among providers." Within this domain, one of our HAIP sites, Parkland Center for Clinical Innovation, used AI to segment their patient population to design tailored clinical programs for clusters of patients (Tamer et al. 2022). This use of AI creates nonfinancial value by improving patient experience and addressing barriers to access.

Third, clinical operations applications are described as "optimizing clinical workflow and capacity throughout [the] care journey." Within this domain, our team at DIHI used AI to predict admissions to the hospital requiring either intermediate or intensive care unit level care (Fenn et al. 2021). This application of AI can improve patient flow within the emergency department, prompting timely inpatient transfers for patients requiring escalation of care and discharge for patients who can safely return home. This use of AI creates financial value by increasing emergency department throughput and nonfinancial value by improving patient experience.

Fourth, clinical analytics applications are described as "improving patient care journey with data at all points of care delivery." This domain overlaps heavily with clinical operations, especially when optimizations to health system operations align with patient care goals. For example, our team at DIHI used AI to identify patients at high risk of postsurgical complications as well as patients at high risk of inpatient mortality (Corey et al. 2018; Brajer et al. 2020). In both these cases, accurate risk stratification can ensure that invasive surgical and medical interventions align with patient goals of care. These uses of AI create nonfinancial value by improving patient experience, but financial value depends on the reimbursement model. In a fee-for-service model, these uses of AI can have a negative financial impact (i.e., by reducing procedures and treatments), whereas in a value-based care model, these uses of AI can create financial value.

Fifth, quality and safety applications are described as "reducing major adverse events with special attention to patient experience and legal compliance." This domain also overlaps heavily with clinical analytics and clinical operations, and the financial impact depends on reimbursement model. For example, our team at DIHI used AI to identify patients at high risk of sepsis as well as patients at high risk of incident HIV (Bedoya et al. 2020; Burns et al. 2022). In both these cases, infections and their resultant complications can be avoided with timely prevention and treatment. These uses of AI create nonfinancial value by improving patient safety and experience, but like other domains, the financial value depends on the reimbursement model. In a fee-for-service model, these uses of AI can have a negative impact, whereas in a value-based cased model, these uses of AI can create financial value.

The final AI delivery domain is value-based care, described as "improving patient outcomes with value-based care models." This domain resolves much of the tension in the prior domains by asserting the reimbursement model. Within this domain, our team at DIHI used AI to predict progression of chronic kidney disease within an accountable care organization population (Sendak, Balu, and Schulman 2017). Patients at high risk of end stage renal disease can be proactively referred to specialty care to initiate interventions that slow disease progression. These use cases create nonfinancial value by improving patient experience and create financial value by reducing costs associated with advanced chronic disease.

The examples above reveal the complexity of capturing value from AI and the role for total mission value metrics that combine financial and nonfinancial measures. In a fee-for-service reimbursement model, the only domain that consistently generates financial value is clinical operations. In a value-based care reimbursement model, a much broader variety of domains generate financial value. However, the efficient scaling and diffusion of AI in healthcare will ultimately be determined by how much total mission value creates real financial returns. In settings that are unable to fully align incentives across payer, hospital, and physician practice, only a limited scope of AI applications will achieve broad adoption.

On-the-Ground Insights

Three on-the-ground insights derived from our work with DIHI and HAIP reveal gaps in evidence relied upon by Sahni and colleagues. First, the benefits of AI integration presented by Sahni and colleagues are highly optimistic both in terms of timing (immediacy of returns) and magnitude (size of returns). Two quantitative estimates are, first, "In our experience, organizations that deploy AI have twice the five-year revenue compound annual growth rate [CAGR] compared with others that do not"; and second, "Our estimates do not include one-time implementation costs, which in our experience are 1.0 to 1.5 times the annual savings." As described above, most health system and provider practice AI use cases do not generate financial value and would not directly increase CAGR. In a recent McKinsey report, five-year annual CAGR was estimated at 3 percent, down from the prior estimate in July 2022 of 7 percent (Patel and Singhal 2023). All health systems face significant financial pressure in the current environment, due to inflation and high labor costs, which are not entirely addressable with AI. It's unclear how health systems that deploy AI would double their CAGR compared to health systems that don't deploy AI.

Existing evidence also does not support the claim that implementation costs for health AI are 1.0 to 1.5 times annual savings. In fact, health information technology (IT) is notorious for high implementation costs that yield minimal returns. For example, while interoperable health IT was estimated to yield $77.8 billion per year in 2005, despite a $30 billion investment by the US government, the impact of electronic health records (EHRs) on health system finances was minimal (Walker et al. 2005; Beauvais et al. 2021). Many health systems saw financial losses from EHR implementations (Adler-Milstein, Green, and Bates 2013). Without well-documented case studies of AI implementations leading to immediate financial value, it's unclear if health systems and physician practices will achieve the described results.

The second problematic gap in evidence relates to the scalability of current health information technology. The authors claim that "all savings estimates are based on the use of technologies available today and assume that adoption reaches full scale." Unfortunately, the authors do not describe how existing AI solutions can be fully scaled to achieve replicable results across settings. Two factors prevent the efficient scaling of current AI solutions across settings. First, current EHR system implementations are highly customized, and significant effort is required to normalize and harmonize data to conduct analyses across sites. Our team estimated the costs of implementing a single model at a single institution to be nearly $220,000 (Sendak, Balu, and Schulman 2017). Redundant effort to scale that single algorithm across all US hospitals would cost nearly $40 million. More recently, we described the significant effort required for interdisciplinary teams to conduct data quality assurance to develop new algorithms within Duke Health as well as externally validate existing algorithms in external settings (Sendak et al. 2022). Integrating AI systems into legacy IT systems in new settings remains a high-cost endeavor. Without infrastructure that normalizes, harmonizes, and monitors data across EHR systems, there are minimal efficiencies of scale for new settings to adopt AI solutions.

Even if the IT infrastructure were in place to scale an AI solution, organizations must adapt to effectively use and benefit from the technologies.

In 2018, our collaborator Madeleine Elish described Sepsis Watch, an AI-driven sepsis detection system, as *sociotechnical* to emphasize the ways in which the technology and social environment interacted to shape use of the AI system in practice (Elish 2018). Since that time, we regularly engage social scientists in our work to help surface change management opportunities and challenges to ensure successful AI integration (Elish and Watkins 2020; Kellogg, Sendak, and Balu 2022). Unfortunately, our experience building and integrating AI solutions across settings reveals that these technologies are not "turn-key," and significant effort is required from transdisciplinary teams to enable successful organizational adoption.

The final gap relates to organizational characteristics associated with AI software adoption. Sahni and colleagues claim, "Hospitals have piloted AI and are beginning to scale adoption in some domains, with larger hospitals having done more than smaller hospitals." Our own work reveals that health system size is not a factor driving AI adoption. Use of AI is highly concentrated within academic medical centers (AMCs), which only account for 35 percent of hospital admissions in the United States (Burke et al. 2019; Sendak et al. 2020; Price, Sachs, and Eisenberg 2022). Large health systems without internal AI expertise are also more likely to rely on EHR vendors for AI solutions, many of which perform poorly when used in new contexts (Wong et al. 2021). Furthermore, our work with HAIP sites has revealed the importance of centralized AI capabilities and organizational governance structures to ensure safe and effective adoption of AI. This best practice is most mature within AMCs that have significant internal AI development and integration expertise.

Overcoming the Activation Energy

To overcome the challenges listed above, we present multiple potential organizational and policy ("seismic") interventions. First, there are high returns to increasing investment in sociotechnical research of AI integrations in healthcare. There is value at both the policy level (i.e., increases in public sector research funding) and at the organizational level (i.e., sustained investment in social science roles). For example, three systematic reviews of randomized control trials (RCTs) evaluating AI products in healthcare were published between October 2021 and September 2022 (Plana et al. 2022; Lam et al. 2022; Zhou et al. 2021). The reviews included 95 studies across 29 countries. Only 15 AI products were validated in RCTs in the US leveraging broadly available data platforms, including EHR systems and radiology imaging data. Of those AI products, sociotechnical research was conducted for two. A team at PennMedicine conducted several studies examining clinician perspectives of an AI system used to prompt serious illness care conversations for patients with cancer, and multiple sites examined organizational factors related to adoption of an AI system to help triage patients with chest pain in the emergency department (Parikh et al. 2022a, 2022b; Gesell et al. 2018; Bean et al. 2021). Without including sociotechnical research as a standard component of AI development and validation, positive results are unlikely to be replicable in new organizational contexts.

Second, technical and regulatory structures could ensure quality control of AI used by health systems and physician practices. As described above, current EHR systems do not facilitate the efficient diffusion of AI across sites. A market failure currently incentivizes health systems to rely on AI solutions provided by EHR vendors, which often perform poorly (Sendak, Price, and Balu 2022; Wong et al. 2021). Even if a best-in-class solution emerges, integration costs prevent efficient scaling. National infrastructure investment could upgrade the current health IT ecosystem to enable rapid scaling across sites. Similarly, standards and regulation could ensure that AI solutions are validated within health systems and physician practices prior to use. Regulators such as the Office of the National Coordinator could require adoption of this best practice for health IT certification, and third-party accreditation organizations, such as the Joint Commission, can ensure that health systems adopt this best practice as part of organizational governance efforts.

Third, capacity-building programs could upskill the healthcare workforce to effectively use AI. Programs that target individual clinicians, such as our DIHI Clinical Research and Innovation Scholarship, can be scaled across clinical training sites to engage more clinicians in AI product development (Sendak et al. 2021). Similarly, programs that equip organizational leaders, such as HAIP, can equip teams of interdisciplinary professionals to rapidly enhance organizational governance of AI. Funding for this training from the public sector could ensure that the existing digital divide does not widen. Without public sector intervention, AI products will largely remain within the ivory tower of highly resourced AMCs.

Conclusion

In their analysis, Sahni and colleagues estimate the total potential savings from AI in healthcare to be $200 billion to $360 billion annually. While we agree that the opportunity to improve healthcare using AI is enormous, our experiences through DIHI and HAIP reveal a more complex picture. In this comment, we present gaps in evidence that must be addressed to ensure that AI solutions are scalable across sites. We also present policy and organizational interventions that could unlock the value of AI in healthcare. Without coordinated investments in sociotechnical research, technical and regulatory structures, and capacity-building programs, the potential benefits of AI in healthcare will remain out of reach for health systems and physician practices.

References

Adler-Milstein, J., C. E. Green, and D. W. Bates. 2013. "A Survey Analysis Suggests That Electronic Health Records Will Yield Revenue Gains for Some Practices and Losses for Many." *Health Affairs* (Project Hope) 32 (3): 562–70. http://content .healthaffairs.org/content/32/3/562.full.pdf.

Bean, G., U. Krishnan, J. R. Stone, M. Khan, and A. Silva. 2021. "Utilization of Chest Pain Decision Aids in a Community Hospital Emergency Department: A Mixed-Methods Implementation Study." *Critical Pathways in Cardiology* 20 (4): 192–207.

Beauvais, B., C. S. Kruse, L. Fulton, R. Shanmugam, Z. Ramamonjiarivelo, and M. Brooks. 2021. "Association of Electronic Health Record Vendors with Hospital Financial and Quality Performance: Retrospective Data Analysis." *Journal of Medical Internet Research* 23 (4): e23961.

Bedoya, A. D., J. Futoma, M. E. Clement, K. Corey, N. Brajer, A. Lin, M. G. Simons, M. Gao, M. Nichols, S. Balu, K. Heller, M. Sendak, and C. O'Brien. 2020. "Machine Learning for Early Detection of Sepsis: An Internal and Temporal Validation Study." *JAMIA Open* 3 (2): 252–60.https://www.ncbi.nlm.nih.gov/pmc /articles/PMC7382639/.

Bellantoni, J., E. Clark, J. Wilson, J. Pendergast, J. M. Pavon, H. K. White, D. Malone, W. Knechtle, and A. Jolly Graham. 2022. "Implementation of a Telehealth Video-conference to Improve Hospital-to-Skilled Nursing Care Transitions: Preliminary Data." *Journal of the American Geriatrics Society* 70 (6): 1828–37.

Brajer, N., B. Cozzi, M. Gao, M. Nichols, M. Revoir, S. Balu, J. Futoma, J. Bae, N. Setji, A. Hernandez, and M. Sendak. 2020. "Prospective and External Evaluation of a Machine Learning Model to Predict In-Hospital Mortality of Adults at Time of Admission." *JAMA Network Open* 3 (2): e1920733–14. https://jamanetwork.com /journals/jamanetworkopen/fullarticle/2760438.

Burke, L. G., D. Khullar, J. Zheng, A. B. Frakt, E. J. Orav, and A. K. Jha. 2019. "Comparison of Costs of Care for Medicare Patients Hospitalized in Teaching and Nonteaching Hospitals." *JAMA Network Open* 2 (6): e195229.

Burns, C. M., L. Pung, D. Witt, M. Gao, M. Sendak, S. Balu, D. Krakower, J. L. Marcus, N. Lance Okeke, and M. E. Clement. 2022. "Development of an Human Immunodeficiency Virus Risk Prediction Model Using Electronic Health Record Data from an Academic Health System in the Southern United States." *Clinical Infectious Diseases* 76 (2): 299–306. https://academic.oup.com/cid/article-abstract /76/2/299/6705475.

Corey, K. M., S. Kashyap, E. Lorenzi, S. A. Lagoo-Deenadayalan, K. Heller, K. Whalen, S. Balu, M. T. Heflin, S. R. McDonald, M. Swaminathan, and M. Sendak. 2018. "Development and Validation of Machine Learning Models to Identify High-Risk Surgical Patients Using Automatically Curated Electronic Health Record Data (Pythia): A Retrospective, Single-Site Study." *PLoS Medicine* 15 (11): e1002701. https://journals.plos.org/plosmedicine/article?id=10.1371/journal.pmed.1002701.

Duke Health. 2023. "Facts & Statistics." https://corporate.dukehealth.org/who-we -are/facts-statistics.

Duke Institute for Health Innovation. 2021. "Health AI Partnership: An Innovation and Learning Network for Health AI Software." December 23, 2021. https://dihi .org/health-ai-partnership-an-innovation-and-learning-network-to-facilitate -the-safe-effective-and-responsible-diffusion-of-health-ai-software-applied-to -health-care-delivery-settings/.

Elish, M. C. 2018. "The Stakes of Uncertainty: Developing and Integrating Machine Learning in Clinical Care." *Ethnographic Praxis in Industry Conference* 2018 (1):

364–80. https://anthrosource.onlinelibrary.wiley.com/doi/full/10.1111/1559-8918
.2018.01213.

Elish, M. C., and E. A. Watkins. 2020. "Repairing Innovation: A Study of Integrating AI in Clinical Care." *Data & Society* Sep 25: 1–62. https://datasociety.net/wp
-content/uploads/2020/09/Repairing-Innovation-DataSociety-20200930–1.pdf

Fenn, A., C. Davis, D. M. Buckland, N. Kapadia, M. Nichols, M. Gao, W. Knechtle,
S. Balu, M. Sendak, and B. Jason Theiling. 2021. "Development and Validation of
Machine Learning Models to Predict Admission from Emergency Department to
Inpatient and Intensive Care Units." *Annals of Emergency Medicine* 78 (2): 290–
302. https://www.annemergmed.com/article/S0196-0644(21)00161-X/fulltext

Gesell, S. B., S. L. Golden, A. T. Limkakeng, C. M. Carr, A. Matuskowitz, L. M.
Smith, and S. A. Mahler. 2018. "Implementation of the HEART Pathway: Using
the Consolidated Framework for Implementation Research." *Critical Pathways
in Cardiology* 17 (4): 191–200.

Kellogg, K. C., M. Sendak, and S. Balu. 2022. "AI on the Frontlines." *MIT Sloan
Management Review* 63 (4): 44–50. https://sloanreview.mit.edu/article/ai-on-the
-front-lines/.

Krol, M. L., C. Allen, L. Matters, A. J. Graham, W. English, and H. K. White. 2019.
"Health Optimization Program for Elders." *Journal of Nursing Care Quality* 34
(3): 217–22.

Lam, T. Y. T., M. F. K. Cheung, Y. L. Munro, K. M. Lim, D. Shung, and J. J. Y.
Sung. 2022. "Randomized Controlled Trials of Artificial Intelligence in Clinical
Practice: Systematic Review." *Journal of Medical Internet Research* 24 (8): e37188.

Parikh, R. B., C. R. Manz, M. N. Nelson, C. N. Evans, S. H. Regli, N. O'Connor,
L. M. Schuchter, L. N. Shulman, M. S. Patel, J. Paladino, and J. A. Shea. 2022a.
"Clinician Perspectives on Machine Learning Prognostic Algorithms in the Routine Care of Patients with Cancer: A Qualitative Study." *Supportive Care in Cancer*
30 (5): 4363–72.

Parikh, R. B., C. R. Manz, M. N. Nelson, W. Ferrell, Z. Belardo, J. S. Temel, M. S.
Patel, and J. A. Shea. 2022b. "Oncologist Perceptions of Algorithm-Based Nudges
to Prompt Early Serious Illness Communication: A Qualitative Study." *Journal of
Palliative Medicine* 25 (11): 1702–7.

Patel, N., and S. Singhal. 2023. "What to Expect in US Healthcare in 2023 and
Beyond." McKinsey & Company, January 9, 2023. https://www.mckinsey.com
/industries/healthcare/our-insights/what-to-expect-in-us-healthcare-in-2023
-and-beyond.

Plana, D., D. L. Shung, A. Λ. Grimshaw, A. Saraf, J. J. Y. Sung, and B. H. Kann.
2022. "Randomized Clinical Trials of Machine Learning Interventions in Health
Care." *JAMA Network Open* 5 (9): e2233946.

Price, W. N., R. Sachs, and R. S. Eisenberg. 2022. "New Innovation Models in Medical AI." *99 Washington University Law Review* 1121. https://ssrn.com/abstract
=3783879.

Sendak, M. P., S. Balu, and K. A. Schulman. 2017. "Barriers to Achieving Economies of Scale in Analysis of EHR Data. A Cautionary Tale." *Applied Clinical
Informatics* 8 (3): 826–31. https://www.thieme-connect.com/products/ejournals
/abstract/10.4338/ACI-2017-03-CR-0046.

Sendak, M. P., J. D'Arcy, S. Kashyap, M. Gao, M. Nichols, K. Corey, W. Ratliff, and
S. Balu. 2020. "A Path for Translation of Machine Learning Products into Healthcare Delivery." *European Medical Journal Innovations*. January 27, 2020. https://
www.emjreviews.com/innovations/article/a-path-for-translation-of-machine
-learning-products-into-healthcare-delivery/.

Sendak, M. P., M. Gao, W. Ratliff, K. Whalen, M. Nichols, J. Futoma, and S. Balu.

2021. "Preliminary Results of a Clinical Research and Innovation Scholarship to Prepare Medical Students to Lead Innovations in Health Care." *Healthcare* 9 (3):100555.

Sendak, M. P., N. Price, and S. Balu. 2022. "A Market Failure Blocks Efficient Diffusion of AI Software for Health." *STAT News*, May 24, 2022. https://www.stat news.com/2022/05/24/market-failure-preventing-efficient-diffusion-health-care -ai-software/.

Sendak, M., G. Sirdeshmukh, T. Ochoa, H. Premo, L. Tang, K. Niederhoffer, et al. 2022. "Development and Validation of ML-DQA—A Machine Learning Data Quality Assurance Framework for Healthcare." *Proceedings of Machine Learning Research* (182): 741–59. https://arxiv.org/abs/2208.02670.

Tamer, Y. T., A. Karam, T. Roderick, and S. Miff. 2022. "Know Thy Patient: A Novel Approach and Method for Patient Segmentation and Clustering Using Machine Learning to Develop Holistic, Patient-Centered Programs and Treatment Plans." *NEJM Catalyst* August 23, 2022. https://catalyst.nejm.org/doi/full/10.1056/CAT .22.0084.

Walker, J., E. Pan, D. Johnston, J. Adler-Milstein, D. W. Bates, and B. Middleton. 2005. "The Value of Health Care Information Exchange and Interoperability." *Health Affairs* 24 (Suppl1): W5-10–W5-18.

Wong, A., E. Otles, J. P. Donnelly, A. Krumm, J. McCullough, O. DeTroyer-Cooley, J. Pestrue, M. Phillips, J. Konye, C. Penoza, M. Ghous, and K. Singh. 2021. "External Validation of a Widely Implemented Proprietary Sepsis Prediction Model in Hospitalized Patients." *JAMA Internal Medicine* 181 (8): 1065–70.

Zhou, Q., Z.-H. Chen, Y.-H. Cao, and S. Peng. 2021. "Clinical Impact and Quality of Randomized Controlled Trials Involving Interventions Evaluating Artificial Intelligence Prediction Tools: A Systematic Review." *NPJ Digital Medicine* 4 (1): 154.

Health Data Platforms

Sendhil Mullainathan and Ziad Obermeyer

3.1 Introduction

Clinical medicine is ripe for transformation by artificial intelligence. The field draws a wide range of highly intelligent people, motivated both by social impact and by the chance to profit from an industry that accounts for 20 percent of US gross domestic product. The health care system also has myriad known inefficiencies in human decision making, the correction of which could create enormous social value. And it produces exabytes of data every year that could easily be used to train useful algorithms.

What then accounts for the conspicuous lack of AI deployed in clinics and hospitals today? Commonly cited factors for this—and many other problems in the health care system—are misaligned financial incentives, regulatory barriers, and behavioral factors. While we are not blind to the challenges these factors present, here we argue for another: the lack of accessible clinical data. We begin by discussing a concrete use case for clinical AI: a tool to help physicians test for heart attack (acute coronary syndromes) in the emergency setting. We then discuss the major barrier to implementing

Sendhil Mullainathan is the Roman Family University Professor of Computation and Behavioral Science at the University of Chicago and a research associate of the National Bureau of Economic Research.

Ziad Obermeyer is an associate professor and Blue Cross of California Distinguished Professor at the School of Public Health, University of California, Berkeley, and a faculty research fellow of the National Bureau of Economic Research.

Mullainathan and Obermeyer are cofounders and hold substantial equity stakes in Dandelion Health, a for-profit entity discussed in this chapter that seeks to promote data access for AI tools in the health care industry. For acknowledgments, sources of research support, and disclosure of the authors' material financial relationships, if any, please see https://www.nber.org/books-and-chapters/economics-artificial-intelligence-health-care-challenges/health-data-platforms.

this tool: data. Finally, we make the case for new mechanisms that connect researchers and clinical product developers to health data.

3.2   Testing for Heart Attack in the Emergency Department (ED)

In recent work, we study how physicians arrive at an important diagnostic decision: whether to test a patient for heart attack, new blockages in the coronary arteries supplying the heart (Mullainathan and Obermeyer 2022a). Patients with heart attack need urgent treatment: untreated blockages can cause heart failure and chronic pain (angina), or arrythmia and sudden death. Blockages cannot be diagnosed from symptoms alone. For example, the most common symptom, chest pain, could also be the result of a pinched nerve or acid reflux, for example. And while the laboratory tests and electrocardiograms (ECGs) done in the ED can be suggestive of blockage, they are not conclusive. As such, physicians rely on an invasive procedure, cardiac catheterization, which can be performed either directly or after a lower-cost stress test. Since these tests are costly, they are applied only when the probability of a heart attack is judged to be sufficiently high.

Central to our approach is a set of tools from the field of machine learning. Because the value of a test depends on the likelihood it will come back positive, the testing decision can be cast as a prediction problem, where machine learning techniques can be profitably applied (Agrawal, Gans, and Goldfarb 2018; Kleinberg et al. 2015). In deciding whom to test, the physician must in effect form a prediction. A test sure to come back negative is a waste; except at the extreme, the value of a test increases with the probability it will come back positive. As such, efficient testing is grounded in effective predicting. By providing explicit predictions, algorithms provide a natural benchmark against which actual decisions can be contrasted. We thus view testing for heart attack as both an important problem in its own right and as a model system for applying machine learning to study diagnostic judgments more generally.

We implement our approach on electronic health record (EHR) data from a large academic medical center. A subset of these is used to train an ensemble machine learning model that uses thousands of variables to predict whether a given test will reveal a coronary blockage. In addition, we build a cost effectiveness model that, for a set of patients at a given predicted risk, calculates the implied cost of a life year for testing that set, based on known benefits and costs of treatment. To check the generality of our results, we replicate them in a 20 percent nationwide sample of ED visits by Medicare beneficiaries. These data, based on insurance claims, are less detailed. But because they are nationally representative, they allow us to explore the relevance of our results for health policy.

We first examine those patients whom physicians choose to test. Our strategy is to use the algorithm's risk predictions to identify *potentially* low-risk patients, in whom testing might not be useful. We then look at *realized* test results to see who was right—the algorithm or the physician. This allows us to calculate the actual value of testing ex post, as a function of predicted risk ex ante, and identify predictably low-value testing. The value of testing is typically adjudicated on the basis of its average yield, and in our setting, the average test has an implied cost effectiveness of $89,714 per life year. At typical US life-year valuations of $100–150,000 (Neumann, Cohen, and Weinstein 2014), this would be considered cost effective. But this aggregate statistic hides a great deal of highly inefficient testing: binning patients by predicted risk reveals that, at a threshold of $150,000 per life year, 62 percent of tests should be cut based on predicted risk. The bottom bin of tests is extremely cost ineffective: $1,352,466 per life year. For comparison, biologics for rare diseases (some of the least cost-effective technologies that health systems sometimes pay for) are typically estimated at around $300,000 per quality adjusted life year.

Even the second-lowest bin is very cost ineffective at $318,603 dollars per life year. By contrast, in the highest-risk quintile bins, tests cost only $46,017 per life year, comparable with cost-effective interventions like dialysis.

The existence of overtesting is not surprising. But as an emerging economics literature suggests, it often coexists with undertesting. In particular, doctors both overtreat low-risk patients and undertreat high-risk patients in a way that suggests errors in diagnostic judgment, and underuse may be at least as consequential as overuse, as has been previously suggested (Currie and MacLeod 2017). In our data, we find that among patients in the highest decile of predicted risk, where testing would appear to be very cost effective, only 38.3 percent are actually tested. This fact raises the possibility of undertesting—but does not fully establish it. The key econometric problem is that we do not know what *would have* happened if we tested these patients.

To answer this question, we look to new data, on major adverse cardiac events in the 30 days after the patient's ED visit that suggest undiagnosed and untreated heart attack. We find that in the highest-risk bin, untested patients go on to have an adverse cardiac event rate of 15.6 percent, high enough for clinical guidelines to conclude they should have been tested. We also leverage exogenous variation in who is tested—some ED shifts test patients more than others—to simulate an experiment, in which a patient is more or less likely to be tested for reasons unrelated to their actual risk. This shows that the highest-risk patients—and only the highest-risk patients—who arrive during the highest-testing shifts have significantly lower mortality (2.5 percentage points, or 32 percent). In contrast, when we look on average, across all patients, without the benefit of machine learning predictions, there is no effect: increasing testing has no statistically significant effect on health outcomes, matching what is often called "flat of the curve" health care.

3.3   Barriers to Implementation of AI Tools

By identifying ex ante which patients ought not to be tested, algorithmic predictions pave the way for targeted interventions to increase the efficiency of testing prospectively. Our current efforts to implement this algorithm as a clinical decision aid have given us insights into why such algorithms are not more widespread.

It is first important to note which barriers are unlikely to pose important barriers. As our results on over- and undertesting above illustrate, such an algorithm would be of great interest to health systems irrespective of their financial incentives. Consider the case of a purely profit-motivated health system that placed no weight on improved patient outcomes. If such a system were paid under a traditional fee-for-service plan, they would be highly incentivized to implement the algorithm to increase testing of high-risk patients: these patients are highly profitable, because they are the most likely to generate the complex procedures and intensive care needs that are major contributors to hospitals' bottom lines (Abelson and Creswell 2012); they are certainly more profitable than a negative test. If by contrast such a system were paid under a risk-based (capitated) model, they too would be highly incentivized to implement the algorithm to reduce testing of low-risk patients: under widely accepted cost-effectiveness rules, about two-thirds of all tests could be cut using information available at the time of the physician's decision.

Regulatory factors are another commonly cited reason that clinical AI is not more widely deployed. But, as recent scholarship demonstrates, the Food and Drug Administration's regulatory approach cannot be a binding constraint: it has approved hundreds of software and AI devices over the past decade (Stern 2022). Finally, behavioral barriers to adoption are widely believed to be common. But in our ongoing experience designing the rollout of the tool in a large hospital system in the setting of a large-scale randomized trial, physicians are eager to adopt tools that improve their own performance. The important caveat is that they must first be convinced, in a data-driven way, that the tools will help. We are addressing these very reasonable concerns by performing in-depth review of individual cases, particularly those with poor patient outcomes, where the algorithm's predictions might have helped.

Rather, we believe the most significant barrier to development and implementation of such algorithms is data. It is instructive to consider how we gained access to the data we needed to build the original algorithm described above. Building up the dataset took years of effort: to identify where the data were housed, clean it, and extract it. Creating the data frame itself— establishing the sample and exclusion criteria, creating the key study outcomes, developing a data-driven definition for missed heart attack, etc.— demanded both deep medical knowledge and careful applied microeconomic data work. Merging in the ECG waveforms was particularly challenging: after identifying the source system and securing access, we discovered the waveforms were stored only as a PDF image file. So we had to write the code to extract the numeric time series from the image.

Even this painstaking work depended on solving a host of logistical issues regarding data access, which are difficult for many researchers to overcome. The EHR data was accessible only because one of us was, at the time, an employee of the academic hospital from which the data were sourced. This arrangement is the norm: data are completely inaccessible to those who do not have the good fortune to be administratively based within a given hospital—even faculty members at universities affiliated with the hospital are typically ineligible, meaning that economists or computer scientists wishing to access data at their university's hospital must first identify a collaborator employed by that hospital. For example, at the time we began the work for the project described above, we were both faculty members at the same university, but only one of us had access to the data—an idiosyncratic result of being on paper an employee of one of the university's affiliated hospitals. Any analyst we wished to use to assist on the project needed to be hired as an employee of the hospital system, meaning that grant funding needed to be obtained and housed at the hospital in question. Taken together, these restrictions provide a major obstacle to cross-disciplinary work, and were a major reason that the work underlying the paper took over eight years to complete.[6]

3.4   The Need for Health Data Platforms

Scientific fields need data to grow and thrive. In economics, the availability of stock market data created the field of quantitative finance; the Medicare claims data hosted at the National Bureau of Economic Research are the foundation of our current understanding of the healthcare system. In computer science, datasets like DARPA's early efforts with Canadian Hansards data, to the recent examples of the Netflix Prize, MNIST, ImageNet, LFW, One Billion Words, and others underlie unprecedented recent progress in translation, sentiment analysis, object and facial recognition, and other tasks (Donoho 2017).

In medicine, by contrast, well-connected researchers are lucky enough to have access to health data by virtue of their employment status or personal connections. Access for everyone else is laborious, costly, time consuming, or just impossible. But it is clearly inefficient for only a small group of in-house researchers to have access to data. In addition to a simple numbers game, where discoveries are more likely to be made if more researchers are taking

---

6. An honest accounting of the project timeline would place a still larger share of the blame on both authors.

shots on goal, there is also misallocation: in machine learning in particular, hospitals are unlikely to win the war for talent when competing with the deep resources of technology companies. And researchers based at well-resourced academic hospitals are likely to work on problems that concern them and their patient populations, while the needs of other populations may be ignored (Kaushal, Altman, and Langlotz 2020).

A commonly cited concern is the protection of patient privacy. But given the many technical solutions to this problem, from sophisticated deidentification methods to highly secure cloud environments, this cannot be the only barrier. Rather, we believe the problem is incentives. Open data are a classic public good: market forces do not favor their creation. While they have enormous benefit to everyone in the long run—patients, health systems, industry—no single actor has a strong incentive to act (Hill, Stein, and Williams 2020; Price and Cohen 2019).

3.5   Emerging Solutions: A Data Platform for Academic Research

We close by highlighting two health data platforms on which we have worked. The first, Nightingale Open Science, is a nonprofit platform to catalyze research (Mullainathan and Obermeyer 2022b). Thanks to philanthropic funding, Nightingale supports the creation of previously unseen datasets, in collaboration with health systems around the world. It then makes the deidentified datasets available to a diverse, global community of researchers on a secure cloud platform. By focusing on data that link medical images with real patient outcomes, the platform aims to foster groundbreaking research into common tasks at the intersection of computation and medicine.

Nightingale's datasets focus on medical imaging data: ECGs, x-rays and CT scans, digital pathology images, etc. Medical images are rich sources of signal about patient health—so rich that doctors are unlikely to make full use of all the information. By contrast, most EHR data (e.g., diagnoses, procedures, text-based notes) are actually produced by doctors and thus more likely to be used effectively. Standardization of imaging protocols across time and place means that a chest x-ray in India looks much like an x-ray in San Francisco. While there is of course some variation across sites and equipment manufacturers, this is small compared to the practice- and system-level variation that affects how diagnoses and other data are captured. Technical tools and legal frameworks for deidentification of medical images exist (e.g., HIPAA in the US, and many other countries' legal frameworks permit sharing). Different types of imaging present different challenges—an ECG is a simple numeric time series, while a head MRI could allow facial reconstruction—but these challenges are increasingly tractable with a robust set of tools.

These datasets were built collaboratively with a range of health systems from around the world. Diversity of data is a key consideration, given the nonrepresentative nature of many current datasets used to build algorithms. In the San Francisco Bay Area, for example, Nightingale partners with a leading academic medical center, and also a far less well-resourced county hospital system. Abroad, partners include the largest hospital in Taiwan, and will soon expand to partnerships in Cameroon and Tamil Nadu.

3.6   Emerging Solutions: A Data Platform for AI Product Development

The second platform, Dandelion Health, is a for-profit platform to cata- lyze AI product development. It is perhaps surprising that market forces have not solved the problem of data access in the private sector, given the large financial incentives to build AI products. While there are several differ- ent types of efforts underway to apply AI to medical datasets, these efforts are limited in several ways. First, several consortia have formed to pool EHR data across large hospital systems. But the center of gravity of those efforts is providing insights and analytics to life sciences companies, in the hopes of capturing a share of the large budgets associated with drug development, rather than AI product development. As a result, high-dimensional imag- ing and waveform data are typically absent, and complex questions about ownership of intellectual property derived from the data remain unresolved. Second, academic medical centers are beginning to partner with companies, or in some cases spinning off new ventures themselves. But these ventures are in practice limited by the complex, laborious approach to contracting, intellectual property, and data access. In addition, the unusual and nonrep- resentative nature of both the populations served by tertiary and quaternary centers, and the care practices in those centers, hampers generalizability. Third, technology companies are beginning to invest heavily in medical data, but of course their goal is to monopolize it for their own purposes, rather than to let market forces accelerate broad product development.

We do not mean to argue that such efforts are doomed to failure: many of them have the potential to produce exciting, innovative tools to improve clinical care. But they are unlikely to unlock the market forces that typically drive innovation in other sectors at scale, either because their focus is not on AI or because data access remains limited by design.

The goal of Dandelion Health is to create the largest and highest-quality AI-ready training dataset in the world, and to become the first end-to-end product development platform for clinical AI. Dandelion has agreements with up to five massive US health systems that allow for access to the uni- verse of clinically generated data: structured EHR data (including labs, vital signs, insurance claims data, etc.) but also notes, radiology and pathology images, neurology and cardiology waveforms, and so on.

A key challenge in building up these datasets is the complexity of stor- age and retrieval of high-dimensional data at health systems. While tabular EHR data have been largely standardized thanks to large vendors, imaging and waveform data are another story entirely. The data are scattered across multiple different vendor storage systems, and hospitals are often restricted by contracts with vendors that impose high per-image costs to retrieve the hospitals' own data. More frustrating still, many hospitals continue to delete or overwrite data because of perceived storage space constraints. If data is the new oil, health systems are actively lighting one of their most precious resources on fire. Solving these problems has given us new insights into why efforts to build up datasets for clinical AI are not more widespread.

After creating the datasets within the partner health systems' environments, Dandelion deidentifies and tokenizes these data, then aggregates and curates data to support the development of new products by third parties. The goal is to securely and ethically realize the value locked in health data—rather than letting them sit unused on health systems' servers—and use them to drive better health for patients.

Naturally, the use of patient data for product development raises legal as well as ethical issues. We have found it useful to start with the Belmont principles, which are the foundation of the ethical practice of research, while considering the complex tradeoffs in this area. The Belmont principles mandate protection of patient privacy, beneficence (doing more good than harm), and justice. These broad principles provided a clear basis for articulating the upside of data sharing for patients, while ensuring respect for their privacy and equity considerations. We feel that a similar cost-benefit tradeoff should be constantly weighed with respect to product development.

To maximize benefits, Dandelion's focus is to improve patient outcomes. As a result, the platform exists exclusively for AI innovators to create solutions that will improve patient care. Another key principle is that products made using Dandelion data should strive to reduce inequities—not exaggerate them. Dandelion conducts its own internal review to ensure that any use cases conform to this high standard, and health system partners review every client request to ensure that the products in question will actually help patients and providers. To minimize costs and risks, Dandelion protects patients' identities and privacy by deidentifying and tokenizing data before it leaves the health systems' environment. Where possible, it goes beyond existing laws to uphold the highest privacy standards. Dandelion does not own the data collected by its health system partners—nor does it sell this data to customers. Dandelion leases access to deidentified data within an encrypted SOC2-certified cloud environment.

3.7   Conclusions

Access to health data is a major bottleneck to progress in clinical AI. By investing in health data platforms to catalyze both research and development, society can realize the huge gains from AI in health that have been long promised but, to date, not delivered.

References

Abelson, R., and J. Creswell. 2012. "Hospital Chain Inquiry Cited Unnecessary Cardiac Work." *New York Times*, August 6, 2012.

Agrawal, A., J. Gans, and A. Goldfarb. 2018. *Prediction Machines: The Simple Economics of Artificial Intelligence*. Boston, MA: Harvard Business Press.

Currie, J., and W. B. MacLeod. 2017. "Diagnosing Expertise: Human Capital, Decision Making, and Performance among Physicians." *Journal of Labor Economics* 35 (1): 18977. https://doi.org/10.1086/687848.

Donoho, D. 2017. "50 Years of Data Science." *Journal of Computational and Graphical Statistics* 26 (4): 745–66. https://doi.org/10.1080/10618600.2017.1384734.

Hill, R., C. Stein, and H. Williams. 2020. "Internalizing Externalities: Designing Effective Data Policies." *AEA Papers and Proceedings* 110: 49–54. https://doi.org/10.1257/pandp.20201060.

Kaushal, A., R. Altman, and C. Langlotz. 2020. "Geographic Distribution of US Cohorts Used to Train Deep Learning Algorithms." *JAMA* 324 (12): 1212–13. https://doi.org/10.1001/jama.2020.12067.

Kleinberg, J., J. Ludwig, S. Mullainathan, and Z. Obermeyer. 2015. "Prediction Policy Problems." *American Economic Review* 105 (5): 491–95. https://doi.org/10.1257/aer.p20151023.

Mullainathan, S., and Z. Obermeyer. 2022a. "Diagnosing Physician Error: A Machine Learning Approach to Low-Value Health Care." *Quarterly Journal of Economics* 137 (2): 1–51. https://doi.org/10.1093/qje/qjab046.

Mullainathan, S., and Z. Obermeyer. 2022b. "Solving Medicine's Data Bottleneck: Nightingale Open Science." *Nature Medicine* 28: 897–99. https://doi.org/10.1038/s41591-022-01804-4.

Neumann, P. J., J. T. Cohen, and M. C. Weinstein. 2014. "Updating Cost-Effectiveness—The Curious Resilience of the $50,000-per-QALY Threshold." *New England Journal of Medicine* 371: 796–97. https://doi.org/10.1056/NEJMp1405158.

Price, W. N., and I. G. Cohen. 2019. "Privacy in the Age of Medical Big Data." *Nature Medicine* 25: 37–43. https://doi.org/10.1038/s41591-018-0272-7.

Stern, A. D. 2022. "The Regulation of Medical AI: Policy Approaches, Data, and Innovation Incentives." NBER Working Paper No. 30639. Cambridge, MA: National Bureau of Economic Research. https://doi.org/10.3386/w30639.

Comment   Tyna Eloundou and Pamela Mishkin

Machine learning tools like large language models (LLMs) have shown remarkable improvements in capabilities in various natural language processing tasks, such as text generation, summarization, and dialogue, over the last few years. However, developing and deploying these models in a responsible and beneficial manner requires access to high-quality and diverse datasets that reflect the domains and contexts of interest. In the field of language

Tyna Eloundou and Pamela Mishkin are researchers at OpenAI.

For acknowledgments, sources of research support, and disclosure of the authors' material financial relationships, if any, please see https://www.nber.org/books-and-chapters/economics-artificial-intelligence-health-care-challenges/comment-health-data-platforms-eloundou.

modeling, recent advances have highlighted the importance of using small, curated datasets to fine-tune LLMs that have been pretrained on massive amounts of unstructured web data (Ouyang et al. 2022). In this comment, we discuss two ways that academic researchers can contribute to the responsible development and deployment of useful machine learning models: creating and governing access to structured datasets (as exemplified by Dandelion and Nightingale) and examining the impacts and policy implications of these systems.

OpenAI is an organization committed to ensuring that artificial general intelligence benefits all of humanity (OpenAI 2018). To this end, we are focused on building and deploying large language models such as GPT-3, Codex, and DALL-E responsibly. To do so, we must carefully track how they are used—and misused—to inform our future research and deployment decisions (Brundage et al. 2022).

One of the key challenges we face is gathering the vast amounts of data needed to train and fine-tune these models. Our current approach consists of two steps: we first train a baseline model with unstructured web data while taking care to ensure a minimum level of quality, and we then fine-tune the models using structured, high-quality data that has been annotated by human contractors. This two-pronged approach is essential for developing models that both have general language understanding and local context (instructions, examples, or prompts) about the use-cases that are presented to them. You can learn more about such techniques via projects like Instruct-GPT (Ouyang et al. 2022), where a language model that has language understanding is trained to better respond to human instructions, and Sparrow (Glaese et al. 2022), where an information-seeking dialogue agent is made to behave according to particular rules and requirements. This is similar to how doctors learn in school: they first receive general education before specializing in particular domains.

The second step of fine-tuning models is the most difficult and demanding, as it requires high-quality and detailed data in domains that often require some level of expertise and domain knowledge. Moreover, creating and using such data in a responsible manner entails addressing several ethical and social issues, such as ensuring fair compensation, informed consent, and representativeness of the data contributors and the potential beneficiaries and stakeholders of the technology. The healthcare field is one of the domains where such issues are particularly salient and challenging, and where there is a significant gap between the availability and quality of data and the needs and expectations of the AI development community.

We believe that initiatives like Dandelion and Nightingale can play a vital role in bridging this gap and facilitating the responsible development and deployment of LLMs in the healthcare domain. Dandelion is a project that partners with large health systems to create and provide access to world-class, high-quality medical datasets that cover various aspects of healthcare, such as diagnosis, treatment, and outcomes. Nightingale is a project that partners with researchers to grant them access to large and diverse datasets and compute resources that can enable them to conduct novel and impactful research in various subfields of healthcare, such as epidemiology, genomics, and clinical trials. We're pleased to see these projects adopting best practices like on data governance and data documentation (Gebru et al. 2021).

We are excited about the potential of these projects to improve the state of the art and the state of the practice of LLMs in the healthcare domain. However, we also recognize that there are still many open and important questions about the impacts and implications of using these systems in real-world settings, such as their effects on the quality and equity of healthcare delivery, their risks and challenges for privacy and security, and their ethical and legal ramifications. We encourage both projects to also provide datasets that can help researchers and practitioners to address these questions, to better understand the realized impacts when models are deployed in the real world.

References

Brundage, Miles, Katie Mayer, Tyna Eloundou, Sandhini Agarwal, Steven Adler, Gretchen Krueger, Jan Leike, and Pamela Mishkin. (2022). "Lessons Learned on Language Model Safety and Misuse." OpenAI. https://openai.com/blog/language-model-safety-and-misuse/.

Gebru, Timnit, Jamie Morgenstern, Briana Vecchione, Jennifer Wortman Vaughan, Hanna Wallach, Hal Daumé III, and Kate Crawford. 2021. "Datasheets for Datasets." *Communications of the ACM* 64 (12): 86–92.

Glaese, Amelia, Nat McAleese, Maja Trębacz, John Aslanides, Vlad Firoiu, Timo Ewalds, Maribeth Rauh, Laura Weidinger, Martin Chadwick, Phoebe Thacker, et al. 2022. "Improving Alignment of Dialogue Agents via Targeted Human Judgements." arXiv preprint. arXiv: 2209.14375.

OpenAI. 2018. "OpenAI Charter." https://openai.com/charter/

Ouyang, Long, Jeff Wu, Xu Jiang, Diogo Almeida, Carroll L. Wainwright, Pamela Mishkin, Chong Zhang, Sandhini Agarwal, Katarina Slama, Alex Ray, et al. 2022. "Training Language Models to Follow Instructions with Human Feedback." arXiv preprint. arXiv: 2203.02155.

Comment   Judy Gichoya

Introduction

In their chapter, Mullainathan and Obermeyer utilize a clinical use case for predicting sudden cardiac death from electrocardiograms (ECGs) to

Judy Gichoya is an associate professor in the Department of Radiology and Imaging Sciences at Emory University School of Medicine.

For acknowledgments, sources of research support, and disclosure of the author's material financial relationships, if any, please see https://www.nber.org/books-and-chapters/economics-artificial-intelligence-health-care-challenges/comment-health-data-platforms-gichoya.

show the role of health data platforms in research and product development. Their clinical case selection is interesting—because sudden cardiac death (SCD) occurs in less than 1 percent of the population, and most deaths occur in low-risk patients, which makes mitigation difficult.

One View Is No View

Current acquisition for health data occurs primarily in healthcare delivery institutions, which often represents a snapshot of patients suffering from an ailment. These data tend to be blind to wellness—yet increasingly these "well" data are continuously collected by commercial entities. For example, in the case of SCD, I noted that smart watches like the Apple Watch collect oxygenation levels, pulse rate, and limited form of ECGs in many patients at various states including young, old, and healthy (Perez et al. 2019; Seshadri et al. 2020; Marcus 2020). A different example is the smart pumps for breast-feeding, which collect and track various breast milk amounts and variations with time of data. Obermeyer agrees that commercial vendors have data that are missing from data platforms, but further notes that such data are limited in their usefulness because they are not linked to patient outcomes. In the case of ECG detection of atrial fibrillation or abnormal rhythms, the commercial vendor is usually unaware of the patient outcome including interventions that occur in the hospital. While this may be the case today, it should not surprise the community when the status quo changes and the commercial vendors purchase clinical data to link and enrich their datasets. Incentives to stimulate public–private partnerships and also include citizen science (who may have ability to download and share their own data) could encourage collaborative work to enrich available health datasets.

Justifying the Need for Health Data Platforms

Obermeyer describes two platforms—the Nightingale open science platform (Mullainathan and Obermeyer 2022) and Dandelion—a commercial data platform for AI development. Dandelion currently supports five large health systems that provide all the raw clinical data and in turn receive clean and structured data. Dandelion provides these data to various stakeholders with a strict focus on products that benefit patients and also shares revenue back to the participating health system. In this paper we observe two variations of health data platforms—one that is problem/dataset driven (Nightingale), while the second one is process driven with a larger amount of data provided through a single contract.

Health data platforms overcome the barriers for data access by shortening the duration to access new data (which usually takes years and is rarely successful); democratizing data access beyond researchers and institutions with more resources; providing a unified data management process including data use agreements; supporting technological advances including cloud integration; and serving as a safe harbor for datasets to be continually improved to prevent dataset expiry. Despite the huge promise of data platforms, their business models rely on locking participants into the platform with no interoperability. This is challenging as these platforms are relatively new in their development and adoption, and not one platform fits multiple end user needs. Moreover, these platforms are owned by startups with high failure rates, which poses a theoretical risk that a selected platform may not be in use in the future.

In organizations with no management structure for interacting and developing these relationships, I anticipate new job titles and managerial units will develop to provide funding and governance and serve as a liaison to ensure compliance and shared benefits flow back to organizations. Cost estimation will remain difficult due to lack of transparency for individual platform components to allow comparison between onsite and cloud servers. As noted by most participants, high infrastructure cost is a barrier to use of healthcare data platforms. A one-year review of our program shows an estimated cost of $100,000 for cloud computing compared to $60,000 for onsite GPU servers. Today, institutions lack capacity in the office of technology transfer to deal with intellectual property and ownership of innovations developed from the shared data.

Incentives Matter

In addition to data sharing incentivized for social good, funders like the National Institutes of Health are mandating data sharing for all funded research. In countries where there is a single payer/universal health care like in Canada, mandates to share all data are easy to enforce compared to multipayer systems. For such cases, health data platforms can be easily harmonized and data easily linked to other data sources like death registries. In a competitive marketplace, commercial partners like insurance providers have enough capital to purchase other data sources and link to the datasets, and these are limited in access. It is important to note that provision of incentives does not equal availability of valuable data, and the process of making data machine learning ready cannot be understated.

Justifying the Status Quo

In 2017, *The Economist* described data as the new oil based on how much data was generated and the combined market forces of the big technology companies in the United States. Coupled with numerous startups working in this space and large venture capital investments for health AI, it should not be a surprise that organizations realized the value of their data, and were reluctant to share it. As the hype has settled and reality set in about the expensive nature of data curation and lack of infrastructure to process and share data easily (as most healthcare organizations do not use cloud solutions and maintain onsite data infrastructure), organizations no longer prioritize data sharing. Legal consequences of data breaches and penalties in the background of ongoing debate that data can never be fully anonymized curb the enthusiasm of organizations to share data. Lastly, a conflict in values—where healthcare organizations are seen to serve the public good versus "evil profit companies" who want to capitalize health data—presents ongoing discourse. Public perception on how data are shared will get worse as more lawsuits and class actions arise when data are not used for the purposes they were intended for, as is the case of the National Health Service in the UK and DeepMind (BBC News 2021).

Concluding Thoughts

To harness the potential of AI for improving healthcare outcomes and reduce costs, data must be democratized and made accessible to researchers and industry. Health data platforms lower this barrier through streamlined data access (agreements and contracting) and improved data quality through curation efforts that provide machine-learning-ready datasets. As organizations decide on which health data platform to adopt, it is important for them to understand the sustainability of the selected platform including the contractual agreements that limit data migration and platform interoperability. To effectively use health data platforms, organizations must develop business units with competency in compliance, data science, finances, intellectual property, and legal expertise of data use agreements. At the society level, incentives must be aligned to promote data sharing and public private partnerships that provide a view on the health side of the patients who interact with healthcare systems.

References

BBC News. 2021. "DeepMind Faces Legal Action over NHS Data Use." October 1, 2021.

The Economist. 2017. "The World's Most Valuable Resource Is No Longer Oil, But Data." May 6, 2017.

Marcus, G. M. 2020. "The Apple Watch Can Detect Atrial Fibrillation: So What Now?" *Nature Reviews Cardiology* 17: 135–36.

Mullainathan, S., and Z. Obermeyer. 2022. "Solving Medicine's Data Bottleneck: Nightingale Open Science." *Nature Medicine* 28: 897–99.

Perez, M. V., K. W. Mahaffey, H. Hedlin, J. S. Rumsfeld, A. Garcia, T. Ferris, V. Balasubramanian, A. M. Russo, A. Rajmane, L. Cheung, et al. 2019. "Large-Scale Assessment of a Smartwatch to Identify Atrial Fibrillation." *New England Journal of Medicine* 381: 1909–17.

Seshadri, D. R., B. Bittel, D. Browsky, P. Houghtaling, C. Drummond, M. Y. Desi, and A. M, Gillinov. 2020. "Accuracy of Apple Watch for Detection of Atrial Fibrillation." *Circulation* 141 (8): 702–3.

Comment   Vardan Papyan, Daniel A. Donoho, and David L. Donoho

Introduction

We congratulate Obermeyer and Mullainathan for spotlighting a new era in medical research. Nightingale Health creates a platform where donations of health data can meet up with donations of machine learning (ML) researcher time and expertise, enabling research that is currently impeded because of legal and other limitations on the sharing of medical research data. Over time, this initiative can lead to entirely new customs in medical research and potentially to the unleashing of a great deal of research energy as traditional barriers to research are shattered.

If data donors and research practitioners take advantage of this new platform en masse, we can envision many new research teams will form, leading to many advances in medical science and also, eventually, in human healthcare.

Our comments mirror the oral remarks we made in person in Toronto in September, and are divided into three sections, based on our three areas of expertise.

Common Task Framework

The platform concept—joining researchers with data—has been proven to work in field after field, across decades. Today's favorite biometric technologies—fingerprint recognition, face recognition, retinal scanning, voice recognition, speech-to-text—were all developed using the so-called Common Task Framework (CTF) in DARPA-sponsored research from the mid-1980s to the mid-2000s. Under CTF, there is a publicly available shared dataset, a defined task, and defined task performance metric, and researchers compete with each other to improve the performance metric. At set intervals, a leaderboard is updated and researchers get to see how others are doing and thereby to understand who is currently "winning" and how far "off the pace" their own efforts are. Periodically, contest ceremonies are conducted, at which winners are proclaimed and some sort of reward is bestowed (Liberman 2010).

As operationalized by DARPA in the 1990s, DARPA contracted with the National Institute of Standards and Technology under the leadership of Jonathon Phillips (Phillips et al. 1998; Christensen and Phillips 2002) to

Vardan Papyan is an assistant professor in the Department of Mathematics, cross-appointed to the Department of Computer Science at the University of Toronto.

Daniel A. Donoho is a neurosurgeon at Children's National Hospital.

David L. Donoho is the Anne T. and Robert M. Bass Professor of Humanities and Sciences and a professor of statistics at Stanford University.

For acknowledgments, sources of research support, and disclosure of the authors' material financial relationships, if any, please see https://www.nber.org/books-and-chapters/economics -artificial-intelligence-health-care-challenges/comment-health-data-platforms-papyan.

create a series of datasets that could be used in a series of annual biometrics challenges. Year after year, researcher performance improved on the various biometrics challenges, typically progressing so that after about five to ten years of such annual challenges, researchers had succeeded in constructing models that approached or exceeded human-level performance.

The same pattern of improvement until reaching human levels of performance was made in challenge after challenge; this held up regardless of the underlying modeling technology. In particular, much of this success pre-dates deep learning models. Specific examples can be found in the excellent work of Isabelle Guyon and collaborators on a variety of challenge problems (Guyon et al. 2004).

We maintain that the recent successes during 2012–2022 in machine vision and natural language processing based on deep learning and its elaborations are merely a continuation of established patterns of successful CTF deployment, with new classes of datasets and a new class of models. From this viewpoint, the big event of the deep learning era was the bright idea of Fei Fei Li and collaborators to create the IMAGENET dataset and the ILSVRC competition, and after that, progress in image recognition proceeded according to customary patterns.

In short we are saying that the "secret sauce" of ML is the CTF rather than the specific technology. From this viewpoint, Yann LeCun made a bigger impact by co-developing the MNIST dataset (with Corinna Cortes) and publishing it than by the specifics of any actual ML models he constructed for use with MNIST. Those early neural nets models have been superseded, but MNIST is still powering research papers today.

From our perspective, Nightingale Health seeks to bring this CTF secret sauce into medical research, and we believe with the right CTF setup, it should be just as successful in medical research as it has been in other fields.

Let us emphasize a key element of the CTF that has always been present in instances where CTF has succeeded. That element is not yet in evidence with Nightingale Health, and including this element should be considered, posthaste.

The so-far missing ingredient is *reward*: for CTF to really work, there needs to be some benefit to the participants who reach the pinnacle of the leaderboard. For example, DARPA gave generous research awards to winners of the annual contest installation; while in the Netflix challenge the winning team split an award of $1,000,000. The rewards don't necessarily need to be purely monetary, but they need to be attention getting and convincing. One can argue that the victory by the University of Toronto team in the ILSVRC 2012 led indirectly to outside financial rewards to the team members, who now enjoy high salaries at major research institutions.

Hence, Nightingale Health could consider ways to offer rewards. These could include not merely rewards for winning a challenge, but also for donating data and for developing a challenge.

To an audience of economists, this point must seem obvious, but among academics this type of essential yet "crass" observation might be omitted because seemingly inappropriate in a "high-minded" discussion. Yet reward has been present (if sometimes implicitly so) in all the success stories of CTF we are aware of.

The Next Decade's Paradigm Will Not Be the Last Decade's Paradigm

Over the last decade, many machine learning systems achieved unprecedented performance, sometimes superhuman, on an assortment of learning tasks arising in a variety of disciplines. In most cases, landmark results were fueled by exponential growth in proprietary image, text, and speech data available to "big tech" hegemons: in the arrival of the cloud, powered by hegemon constructions of massive data centers distributed globally, and, despite the failure of Moore's law at the CPU level, massive performance boosts in individual computing power following widespread adoption of GPU technology. On top of this, there were numerous algorithmic and architectural advances introduced by the deep learning community (Sevilla et al. 2022).

Nightingale's platform aims to bring some of the last decade's innovations into the medical research context. This is exciting, and very promising. However, just as AI researchers who were not employed at hegemons faced roadblocks in exploiting data and computing during the last decade, there may well be, during the coming decade, obstacles for medical researchers and their ML collaborators to follow the last decade's successful roadmap using Nightingale.

For the new platform to fully follow the roadmap of the last decade, Nightingale must provide to its users access to massive computing and massive data. In terms of computing, currently on Nightingale, a GPU hour costs $1. Ideally, Nightingale would allow researchers to use national clusters (e.g., Compute Canada) or university clusters (e.g., Stanford's Sherlock cluster) since these are significantly more affordable to academics. Ideally, Nightingale would also allow nonresearchers to use cloud computing, which often provides GPUs at a lower price point (e.g., preemptable GPUs) and would also allow integration with other cloud computing services. Thus, what has worked previously in empirical ML seems to require that Nightingale broaden its computing strategy.

In terms of data, currently all datasets in Nightingale are labeled; Nightingale seems to be all-in on the paradigm of supervised learning. The supervised learning approach faces two important considerations: getting expert labels on data can be expensive, and there is a radically larger amount of unlabeled data than there is of labeled data.

Since the beginning of this decade, thought leadership in AI has begun to challenge the labeled-data paradigm. In particular, recently reported advances in self-supervised learning seem to show that training deep learning models no longer requires large labeled datasets. To the point for those interested in medicine, recent work (Azizi et al. 2021) has shown the effectiveness of self-supervised learning as a pretraining strategy for medical image classification. Thus, current thought leadership in empirical ML seems to require that Nightingale broaden its data strategy, to diversify its datasets and allow for productive exploitation of unlabeled data.

Medical Datasets and Artificial Intelligence

Nightingale provides an excellent playground for ML scientists to test new methods and algorithms on a well-curated corpus of medical datasets, and allows for the adoption of new datasets after their development. In that way, it may serve to highlight certain particular clinical use cases that are impactful (global ophthalmologic health, chest radiographs for tuberculosis, and so on) and focus the attention of the computational field on optimization for those use cases. However, the two largest challenges to the development of impactful artificial intelligence systems are data exfiltration (i.e., getting data out of the medical context they are currently locked inside, such as a surgeon's video microscope or a hospital electronic medical record) and operationalization of ML models. Platforms functioning in the intermediate step between data exfiltration and productization, such as Nightingale, have a unique opportunity to shape the course of the entire ecosystem.

First, by providing incentives for the development of large, high-quality datasets, and structures to manage terms of use, intellectual property, and compensation, Nightingale enables the use of ML to identify and address important clinical and public health challenges. Nightingale could provide incentives not only for ML researchers to vie for the top of the leaderboard (as described in "Common Task Framework," above), but also for medical stakeholders to develop and contribute deidentified, large unlabeled, sparsely labeled, or coarsely labeled datasets (as in "The Next Decade's Paradigm Will Not Be the Last Decade's Paradigm," above) in selected high-impact areas. These incentives would reward the careful curation and dataset exfiltration from the Health Insurance Portability and Accountability Act of 1996 (HIPAA) domain to the non-HIPAA domain, two principal challenges to the development and deployment of code against data. Incentives could be aligned with the mission of other larger organizations and given in the form of cash or model credits. For example, one could imagine a "Nightingale x PEPFAR Challenge" to generate datasets that support ML applications in HIV/AIDS research.

During dataset development, the sensitive nature of medical data and strict privacy regulations under HIPAA and the EU's General Data Protection Regulation generate significant challenges and costs. Incentives can help encourage and focus efforts to overcome these barriers across institutions.

Furthermore, a transparent, standardized, and open framework for formulating terms of use, intellectual property agreements, and compensation would accelerate institutional participation. Nightingale's incentives could be aligned with the mission of other larger organizations, such as government agencies or healthcare providers, and could be given in the form of cash or model credits.

Second, Nightingale could provide structures and frameworks for model outputs and deployment inputs to promote impact within the public health and healthcare environments. One of the key challenges in the development and deployment of ML algorithms in healthcare is the need to ensure that the models are able to produce reliable, interpretable, and actionable outputs that can be used by healthcare providers and other stakeholders. This involves not only developing and training the models but also ensuring that the outputs are suitable for use in real-world settings.

To address this challenge, Nightingale should provide structures and frameworks to shape the outputs of ML models and receive return inputs from operational deployments. This could involve the development of tools and frameworks to support the deployment of ML models in healthcare settings, as well as mechanisms for monitoring and evaluating the performance and impact of these models.

For example, Nightingale could provide metrics for assessing the accuracy, precision, and interpretability of model outputs. Nightingale could also provide mechanisms for incorporating feedback from healthcare providers and other stakeholders into the model development process, such as mechanisms for soliciting and incorporating user feedback on model performance and outputs.

By providing these structures and frameworks, Nightingale can provide an ML playground that not only allows for academic development and skill building but also promotes the development of ML algorithms that are actionable and impactful in real-world healthcare settings.

Conclusion

The Nightingale platform has the potential to drive significant advances in medical research by bringing together researchers and data donors. By incorporating elements of the successful CTF, such as rewards and leaderboards, Nightingale can encourage participation and drive progress in the field. The ability to perform compute on local clusters would significantly accelerate adoption. In contrast to the supervised datasets currently available, methods that use unsupervised or semisupervised data are gaining in popularity. Nightingale could provide incentives for the development of large, sparsely labeled datasets in selected high-impact areas, and provide structures to shape the outputs of ML models and receive feedback from operational deployments. Positioned at the center of a medical artificial intelligence research workflow, Nightingale has the potential to shape the future of artificial intelligence in healthcare and accelerate innovation in global public health.

References

Azizi, Shekoofeh, Basil Mustafa, Fiona Ryan, Zachary Beaver, Jan Freyberg, Jonathan Deaton, Aaron Loh, Alan Karthikesalingam, Simon Kornblith, Ting Chen, Vivek Natarajan, and Mohammad Norouzi. 2021. "Big Self-Supervised Models Advance Medical Image Classification." Proceedings of the IEEE/CVF International Conference on Computer Vision (ICCV), Montreal, October 10–17.

Christensen, H. I., and P. J. Phillips, eds. 2002. *Empirical Evaluation Methods in Computer Vision*. River Edge, NJ: World Scientific Publishers.

Guyon, I., S. Gunn, A. Ben-Hur, and G. Dror. 2004. "Result Analysis of the NIPS 2003 Feature Selection Challenge." *Advances in Neural Information Processing Systems* 17.

Liberman, Marc. 2010. "Obituary: Fred Jelinek." *Computational Linguistics* 36 (4): 595–99.

Phillips, P. J., H. Wechsler, J. Huang, and P. J. Rauss. 1998. "The FERET Database and Evaluation Procedure for Face-Recognition Algorithms." *Image and Vision Computing* 16 (5): 295–306.

Sevilla J, L. Heim, A. Ho, T. Besiroglu, M. Hobbhahn, and P. Villalobos. 2022. "Compute Trends across Three Eras of Machine Learning." arXiv preprint. arXiv 2202.05924. Feb 11.

The Regulation of Medical AI
Policy Approaches, Data, and Innovation Incentives

Ariel Dora Stern

4.1 Introduction

For those who follow health and technology news, it is difficult to go more than a few days without reading about a compelling new application of artificial intelligence (AI) to healthcare. Applications range from basic science (e.g., understanding protein folding), to translational science (e.g., supporting drug discovery), to improving existing digital offerings (e.g., using machine learning [ML] algorithms to adjust for missing data in whole genome sequencing software), to tools that promise to improve healthcare delivery in myriad ways. Recent work has highlighted and categorized the applications of AI to healthcare delivery and emphasized how contemporary deep learning approaches are likely to transform healthcare (Hinton 2018). The overwhelming majority of applications of AI fall into one of three broad categories: administrative work, diagnosis, and treatment. Table 4.1 provides examples of the types of AI tools that fit into each of these categories.

To make their way into routine healthcare delivery, AI tools for admin-

Ariel Dora Stern is an associate professor of business administration in the Technology and Operations Management Unit at Harvard Business School and is affiliated with the Harvard-MIT Center for Regulatory Science.

The author is grateful to Melissa Ouellet for excellent research and programming support. Boris Babic, Anna Goldenberg, Nicholson Price, Daniel Yong, and participants at the Fall 2022 Economics of Artificial Intelligence Conference provided thoughtful comments and feedback. The author reports sitting on the Scientific Advisory Board of the German Society of Digital Medicine and the Strategic Advisory Board of HumanFirst. From 2020 to 2021 she consulted to the German Federal Ministry of Health on topics that included the regulation and reimbursement of digital medical devices. For acknowledgments, sources of research support, and disclosure of the author's material financial relationships, if any, please see https://www.nber.org/books-and-chapters/economics-artificial-intelligence-health-care-challenges/regulation-medical-ai-policy-approaches-data-and-innovation-incentives.

Table 4.1   **Applications of AI to health care delivery: Examples**

Category	Examples
(1) Administrative work	Provider documentation Order, prescription, coding entry for providers Data entry Scheduling Triaging
(2) Diagnosis	Imaging/pathology review Diagnostic models/symptom analysis Phenotyping Incorporating nontraditional data sources
(3) Treatment	Surgical assistance Individualized/personalized medicine Adherence and health coaching Generating treatment recommendations Digital therapeutics

Source: Adapted from Sanders et al. 2019

istrative work will need to cater to provider preferences, workflows, and other site-specific norms (Sanders et al. 2019). Beyond these practical and design challenges, AI-driven administrative support tools need to comply with data privacy regulations in the jurisdictions in which they are used— most notably, the HIPAA Privacy Rule[1] in the United States and the GDPR[2] in Europe. AI tools for performing or supporting administrative work in healthcare promise to improve the efficiency of healthcare delivery by aiding in clinician note-taking and documentation, scheduling, triaging, ordering medications, and avoiding medication errors—including foreseeable nega-

1. The US Health Insurance Portability and Accountability Act (HIPAA) dates back to 1996. The HIPAA Privacy Rule "establishes national standards to protect individuals' medical records and other individually identifiable health information (collectively defined as "protected health information" [PHI]) and applies to health plans, health care clearinghouses, and those health care providers that conduct certain health care transactions electronically." In addition to requiring "appropriate safeguards" to protect PHI, the rule limits how data can be used/reused without an individual's authorization and gives individuals the right to obtain and examine copies of their own health records. See https://www.hhs.gov/hipaa/for-professionals/privacy/index.html.

2. The European Union's General Data Protection Regulation (GDPR) "lays down rules relating to the protection of natural persons with regard to the processing of personal data and rules relating to the free movement of personal data." The regulation further "protects fundamental rights and freedoms of natural persons and in particular their right to the protection of personal data" and governs the movement of such data within the EU (Art. 1 GDPR, https://gdpr-info.eu/art-1-gdpr). The GDPR specifically recognizes "data concerning health" as its own category and provides specific definitions for health data for the purposes of data protection under the GDPR (https://edps.europa.eu/data-protection/our-work/subjects/health_en).

tive interactions. Importantly, however, administrative support tools rarely qualify as regulated medical products and, conditional on compliance with applicable privacy laws, therefore rarely fall under the jurisdiction of medical product—chiefly, medical device—regulations.

In diagnosis and treatment, however, a large and growing number of AI tools meet the definition of a medical device or that of an in-vitro diagnostic. Those that do are subject to regulation by local authorities, with implications for manufacturers and a more complex set of innovation incentives. This chapter provides a brief background on medical device regulation in the United States and Europe and discusses a few emergent regulatory approaches that are designed to address some of the unique challenges of regulating software as a medical device. It then takes a closer look at regulated AI devices in the United States by identifying such devices in the Food and Drug Administration's (FDA) databases.

The empirical section of this chapter explores regulated, software-based, AI-supported/-driven medical devices ("AI devices") in the United States. By taking advantage of publicly available information about all medical device clearances and associated product summaries, this section uses text analysis to identify AI devices and compare these to other devices in the same medical product areas—including the subset of comparator devices that are themselves software driven. In particular, we characterize AI devices based on the types of firms they originate in and the countries in which they are developed. The chapter also presents summary data on the safety profiles of AI devices, as measured by mandatory adverse event reports and product recalls. Building on descriptive statistics from the US data, the fourth section of this chapter discusses how regulation is likely to shape innovation incentives for (certain types of) AI devices and how both regulatory innovation and regulatory transparency may play a role in the future of regulated AI devices. The chapter concludes with a brief discussion of a forward-looking research agenda.

4.2   Background and Policy Approaches

4.2.1   Medical Device Regulation in the United States

US medical product regulation can be traced back over a century to the Pure Food and Drug Act of 1906. However, modern medical *device* regulation began with the 1976 Medical Device Amendments (MDA) to the 1938 Federal Food, Drug, and Cosmetic Act. The MDA created federal oversight of medical devices for the first time (previously they had been regulated by the states) and established the framework for how medical devices are regulated today. Section 201(h) of the Food, Drug, and Cosmetic Act defines a medical device as:

An instrument, apparatus, implement, machine, contrivance, implant, in vitro reagent, or other similar or related article, including a component part, or accessory which is:

1. recognized in the official National Formulary, or the United States Pharmacopoeia, or any supplement to them,
2. intended for use in the diagnosis of disease or other conditions, or in the cure, mitigation, treatment, or prevention of disease, in man or other animals, or
3. intended to affect the structure or any function of the body of man or other animals, and which does not achieve its primary intended purposes through chemical action within or on the body of man or other animals and which does not achieve its primary intended purposes through chemical action within or on the body of man or other animals and which is not dependent upon being metabolized for the achievement of its primary intended purposes. The term "device" does not include software functions excluded pursuant to section 520(o).[3]

In short, a medical device is a tool for the diagnosis or treatment of disease, which is not a metabolized (biological or pharmaceutical) product.

Current medical device regulations are focused on providing users (including patients, clinicians, provider organizations, and caregivers) reasonable assurance regarding the safety and effectiveness of medical devices. Medical devices are regulated by the FDA's Center for Devices and Radiological Health (CDRH), which uses a risk-based, three-tier classification system for all devices:[4]

- Devices of the lowest risk (Class I) are subject to only general manufacturing controls and typically exempt from needing a premarketing submission/application. These include products such as tongue depressors, condoms, latex gloves, bandages, and surgical masks.
- Moderate risk (Class II) devices are typically regulated through a process called "Premarket Notification" or, more often, the "510(k) process." This process requires a device to demonstrate "substantial equivalence" with one or more already legally marketed devices.[5] Class II devices that do not have a legally marketed "predicate" device can also use a "De Novo" Classification request to come to market if the manufacturer is

3. See https://www.fda.gov/medical-devices/classify-your-medical-device/how-determine -if-your-product-medical-device.

4. See https://www.fda.gov/medical-devices/overview-device-regulation/classify-your -medical-device.

5. A device is considered substantially equivalent if, in comparison to a predicate, it has the same intended use, the same technological characteristics, or the same intended use and has different technological characteristics and does not raise different questions of safety and effectiveness; and the information submitted to FDA demonstrates that the device is as safe and effective as the legally marketed device (https://www.fda.gov/medical-devices/premarket -submissions-selecting-and-preparing-correct-submission/premarket-notification-510k).

able to provide reasonable assurance of safety and effectiveness of the device for the intended use. Subsequent devices can then use a device that came to market through the De Novo process as a predicate in their own ensuing 510(k) applications.

- Finally, devices of the highest risk (Class III) are those that are implantable and/or life sustaining and, as such, require significant evidence of safety and effectiveness to be approved for marketing. With a few exceptions for devices that pre-date the MDA, Class III devices are regulated through a process called "Premarket Approval" or the "PMA process," which is the most rigorous of all pre-market submissions and typically requires evidence from clinical studies. The PMA process is significantly more onerous than the 510(k) process and has been associated with longer periods of regulatory approval for first movers in new medical device product codes. (Stern 2017)

In addition to establishing these regulatory pathways for new medical devices, the MDA created a regulatory pathway for new investigational devices to be studied in human patients, the investigational device exemption (IDE), and established several postmarket requirements and processes—including adverse event reporting requirements—and good manufacturing practices (GMPs). The Safe Medical Devices Act of 1990 filled in additional policy gaps in medical device regulation by authorizing the FDA to order device recalls and impose civil penalties for violations, and improved postmarket surveillance by requiring both manufacturers and user facilities (hospitals, clinics, nursing homes, etc.) to report adverse events associated with the use of specific medical devices.[6] Further, the FDA's Breakthrough Devices Program was created in 2018 to provide patients and healthcare professionals with more timely access to devices that "provide for more effective treatment or diagnosis of life-threatening or irreversibly debilitating diseases or conditions," and as of the end of Q3, 2022, a total of 56 devices with the Breakthrough Device designation had received marketing authorization.[7]

Regardless of the regulatory pathway used, all devices are categorized into three-letter product codes that describe the device's generic category of use. Within a product code, devices are thus very good to excellent substitutes for one another. For example, unique product codes exist for *Coronary Drug-Eluting Stent* (NIQ), *Catheter, Balloon for Retinal Reattachment* (LOG), *Oximeter, Fetal Pulse* (MMA), and *Infusion Safety Management Software* (PHC).[8] Regulation happens at the level of 18 panels of the CDRH Advisory Committee, which are organized by medical specialty (e.g., the Circulatory

6. See https://www.fda.gov/medical-devices/overview-device-regulation/history-medical-device-regulation-oversight-united-states.
7. See https://www.fda.gov/medical-devices/how-study-and-market-your-device/breakthrough-devices-program.
8. See https://www.fda.gov/medical-devices/classify-your-medical-device/product-code-classification-database.

System Devices Panel reviews cardiovascular devices, while the Radiological Devices Panel reviews radiology devices).

For devices that are cleared via the 510(k) or De Novo processes or approved via the PMA process, several public documents are published online at the time that a device receives a positive regulatory decision. These include a device summary for 510(k)-track devices, which "includes a description of the device such as might be found in the labeling or promotional material for the device, including an explanation of how the device functions, the scientific concepts that form the basis for the device" as well as information on "the significant physical and performance characteristics of the device, such as device design, material used, and physical properties," making this document an excellent source of information on a device's key technological characteristics. The PMA process also requires a product-specific summary document, which is made publicly available at the time the device is approved. PMA summary documents also contain information on indications for a device's use and a detailed device description, including "how the device functions, the basic scientific concepts that form the basis for the device, and the significant physical and performance characteristics of the device" in addition to other requirements.[9] The text analysis that follows takes advantage of publicly available product summaries in order to understand and categorize devices' technical content and functionality at scale.

4.2.2   Regulation of Software-Driven Medical Devices

Because US medical device regulation is grounded in legislation from 1976 (the MDA), provisions for thinking about the regulation of software-driven products were not codified for the first several decades. This means that until recently, medical device regulations were woefully mismatched to the special needs and nuances of software products. Specifically, any significant updates to medical devices have historically required new applications to regulators. For a moderate-risk device, there are no regulatory provisions for amending or changing an existing 510(k) clearance—that is "if it is determined the modification is not covered by the current 510(k) a new 510(k) must be submitted."[10] PMA-track devices can only be modified through a PMA supplement, a "submission required for a change affecting the safety or effectiveness of the device for which the applicant has an approved PMA."[11] For example, a software change "that significantly affects clinical functionality

9. See https://www.accessdata.fda.gov/scripts/cdrh/cfdocs/cfcfr/CFRSearch.cfm?FR =814.20.
10. See https://www.fda.gov/medical-devices/premarket-notification-510k/new-510k -required-modification-device.
11. See https://www.fda.gov/medical-devices/premarket-approval-pma/pma-supplements -and-amendments.

or performance specifications" would require a new premarket submission (US FDA 2019).

This policy rigidity and the discreteness of product updates in this context contrast starkly with that of products in consumer technology settings, where software programs are regularly, if not constantly, being improved upon and modified by developers. Nevertheless, a strict interpretation of US regulatory policies would require a new regulatory submission in the event of a modification to an existing software program that improves the accuracy of a diagnosis being made or information being conveyed to clinicians. While some exceptions were made previously for the addressing of safety and security issues associated with medical device software, it was not until 2017 that the FDA published formal regulatory guidance addressing when a manufacturer should submit a 510(k) for a software change to an existing medical device.[12]

There are two primary ways in which software can be included in a medical device. First, the medical device may be software driven in that it is a physical device that is powered by software that is inextricable from the device's functionality, sometimes called "software in a medical device" or SiMD. An example of SiMD would be the software that powers a CT scanner: the hardware device does not work without the software. Alternatively, a medical device may *entirely* software based—that is, the software itself meets the definition of a medical device (including in-vitro diagnostics). This second category is termed "software as a medical device" or SaMD by the International Medical Device Regulators Forum, which defines SaMD as "software intended to be used for one or more medical purposes that perform these purposes without being part of a hardware medical device"— that is, stand-alone software (IMDRF 2013).

In the United States, SaMD products are typically classified as Class II devices and are regulated via the 510(k) or De Novo pathways. However, low-risk products that meet the definition of SaMD often qualify for "enforcement discretion," meaning that the FDA will not enforce regulatory requirements for these software products.[13] In light of the complexity of regulating SaMD products, there have been recent calls for "innovation in regulatory approaches" to further address the unique needs of SaMD (Torous, Stern, and Bourgeois 2022).

One proposed approach to the regulation of SaMD products was considered in the FDA's Digital Health Software Pre-Certification Program (Pre-

---

12. See https://www.fda.gov/media/99785/download.

13. See https://www.fda.gov/media/80958/download. Other sometimes-regulated products include "smart wearables" such as devices manufactured by Fitbit, AliveCor, Garmin, and Apple, which have both medical and consumer applications. Felber and Maciorowski (2023) provide an overview of how such smart wearables are used and regulated in the United States, along with relevant risks and public purpose considerations.

Cert), a pilot program that was first initiated in 2017 and ran until September of 2022.[14] The pilot phase of the program was intended to "help inform the development of a future regulatory model that [would] provide more streamlined and efficient regulatory oversight of software-based medical devices" and included an outline of how FDA might evaluate SaMD products more responsively by focusing on reviewing an "Excellence Appraisal" of the manufacturer's software development practices, as well as review pathway determination, streamlined review, and real-world performance data collection and evaluation.[15] While the program held the promise of being more dynamic—an approach that surely makes sense for medical software—it was ultimately concluded abruptly in September of 2022 after the "FDA encountered challenges with implementing the proposed approach under [its] current statutory authorities." Among other things, the FDA reported that it "was simultaneously unable to pilot the program approaches with a broad sample of devices while also being unable to limit the scope of any resulting device classifications." It noted that certain types of information gathering were hampered by the fact that it "could not require pilot participants to provide information under the pilot that was not otherwise already required under existing statute," however many participants helped voluntarily.[16] Other challenges with the Pre-Cert approach were foreshadowed even before the conclusion of the pilot. For example, researchers found it difficult "to identify a standard measure that differentiated apps requiring regulatory review from those that would not" using publicly available information, including product descriptions (Alon, Stern, and Torous 2020). Thus, while it is almost certainly the case that novel regulatory approaches are needed for SaMD in general and for AI devices in particular, it will likely be difficult to implement such approaches in the absence of formal updates to regulators' statutory authority that take into account the specific and dynamic needs associated with software products.

4.2.3   Medical Device Regulation in the European Union

The regulation of medical devices in European Union (EU) member states bears several similarities to US medical device regulation (including a risk-based framework governing device classification and regulation), but also has many important differences. The EU Medical Device Regulation 2017/745 (MDR)[17] was adopted in 2017 and fully implemented—thereby replacing previous directives and regulations—in May 2021. The MDR defines a medical device as:

---

14. See https://www.fda.gov/media/161815/download.
15. See https://www.fda.gov/media/106331/download.
16. See https://www.fda.gov/media/161815/download.
17. See https://eur-lex.europa.eu/eli/reg/2017/745/2020–04–24.

any instrument, apparatus, appliance, software, implant, reagent, material or other article intended by the manufacturer to be used, alone or in combination, for human beings for one or more of the following specific medical purposes:

- diagnosis, prevention, monitoring, prediction, prognosis, treatment or alleviation of disease,
- diagnosis, monitoring, treatment, alleviation of, or compensation for, an injury or disability,
- investigation, replacement or modification of the anatomy or of a physiological or pathological process or state,
- providing information by means of in vitro examination of specimens derived from the human body, including organ, blood and tissue donations, and which does not achieve its principal intended action by pharmacological, immunological or metabolic means, in or on the human body, but which may be assisted in its function by such means.

In the EU, medical devices undergo a conformity assessment, leading to a CE mark from a notified body (an organization designated by an EU country to assess the conformity of certain products before being placed on the market)[18] and must comply with the EU's General Data Protection Regulation ([EU] 2016/679, GDPR),[19] which "protects fundamental rights and freedoms of natural persons and in particular their right to the protection of personal data" and presents a general and binding framework for processing the personal data of any person within the EU and by any data processor (party) in the EU. Brönneke et al. (2021) provide an overview of regulatory, legal, and market aspects facing digital products, including a more detailed discussion of the application of the MDR and GDPR to digital medical devices.

4.2.4   Data

The empirical section of this chapter explores regulated, software-based, AI-supported, and AI-driven medical devices (henceforward "AI devices")[20] in the United States. By taking advantage of detailed, publicly available information about medical device clearances and associated product summaries, this section uses text analysis to identify AI devices and compare these to other devices in the same medical product areas—including the subset of those comparator devices that are themselves software driven.

One of the first studies to survey FDA-regulated AI devices was Ben-

18. See https://single-market-economy.ec.europa.eu/single-market/goods/building-blocks/notified-bodies_en.

19. See https://gdpr-info.eu/.

20. This study does not distinguish between AI-supported versus (entirely) AI-driven medical devices. For example, a piece of radiology equipment that uses AI to improve image quality (AI-supported) would qualify as an AI device, as would a SaMD product in which the algorithm itself constitutes the entirety of the medical device (fully AI-driven).

jamens, Dhunnoo, and Meskó (2020), which claimed to publish "the first comprehensive and open access database of strictly AI/ML-based medical technologies that have been approved by the FDA." The database, hosted by the Medical Futurist Institute (TMF), included 79 devices as of mid-2022 (but had not been updated since mid-2021).[21] While the data used in this chapter were collected independently, the TMF database provided early clues to inform how to best identify AI devices and which medical specialties are likely to be most relevant for AI applications at present. For example, just two of the devices in the database were regulated through the PMA process for devices of the highest risk; the remainder were brought to market via the 510(k) or De Novo pathways. This is consistent with most SaMD products coming to market through these pathways, as envisioned by the Pre-Cert program. Further, among the devices in the TMF database, over 80 percent are either radiology or cardiology devices, pointing to the outsized representation of these two medical specialties among AI devices. Combined, these facts strongly suggest that focusing just on devices regulated via the 510(k) pathway and the most common regulatory medical specialties including cardiology and radiology should allow us to limit the scope of data collection, while still likely capturing the vast majority of FDA-regulated AI devices. A subsequently published list of AI devices released by the FDA and updated in October 2022 confirmed similar patterns, with just two out of hundreds of AI devices that came to market since 2010 having done so via the PMA pathway.[22] The data assembly strategy and empirical analyses that follow are based on this data-informed approach.

As the basis for our analysis, we downloaded the full 510(k) database for the years 2010 through 2022 Q3.[23] We focused on the eight largest medical specialties (as defined by their respective FDA Advisory Committee Panels): Clinical Chemistry and Toxicology Devices, Cardiovascular Devices, Dental Products, Gastroenterology-Urology Devices, General Hospital and Personal Use Devices, Orthopedic and Rehabilitation Devices, Radiological Devices, and General and Plastic Surgery Devices. This resulted in a total of 38,812 unique device clearances over 13 calendar years, as presented in table 4.2. The 510(k) database includes information on the device type (product code); data about the applicant firm (device manufacturer), such as its name and filing address; the dates on which each application was submitted to regulators; the dates on which each device was cleared by the FDA; and the medical specialty (as assigned to one of the FDA Medical

---

21. List pulled on June 7, 2022, from https://medicalfuturist.com/fda-approved-ai-based
-algorithms.

22. For the most recent list of AI/ML devices from the FDA see https://www.fda.gov/medical
-devices/software-medical-device-samd/artificial-intelligence-and-machine-learning-aiml
-enabled-medical-devices.

23. Data downloaded on October 4, 2002, from https://www.fda.gov/medical-devices/510k
-clearances/downloadable-510k-files.

Device Advisory Committees[24]) associated with the device. We further flag devices that were part of the Breakthrough Devices Program (see section 4.2.1 for more detail).

We merge onto this database two additional sources of information on device outcomes: data on adverse events associated with medical devices, as collected in the FDA's medical device adverse event reporting database (the Manufacturer and User Facility Device Experience or MAUDE database)[25]; and data on medical device recalls—a more definitive indication of a systematic problem with a product—from the FDA's recall database.[26]

The MAUDE database includes all reported adverse events involving medical devices. Notably, the FDA cautions against causal interpretation: a device being involved in an adverse event does not mean that the device *caused* the adverse event. For example, the FDA's website explains:

> The FDA reviews all medical device reports (MDRs) received. The FDA's analysis of MDRs evaluates the totality of information provided in the initial MDR as well as any MDR supplemental reports subsequently provided. The submission of an MDR itself is not evidence that the device caused or contributed to the adverse outcome or event. For example, in certain MDRs, the text of the report may include the word "death" or a related term. However, the MDR would not, and should not, be classified as death unless the reporter believes the patient's cause of death was or may have been attributed to the device or the device was or may have been a factor in the death.[27]

Nevertheless, the MAUDE database is useful as a surveillance tool, and it provides regulators and researchers with a quantitative and qualitative overview of potential safety issues associated with devices.

When such safety issues are found to be systematic, the manufacturer may issue a recall, under the FDA's oversight, which would remove the device from the market (either indefinitely or until remedial action can be taken) due to a problem with a medical device that violates FDA law. The types of "correction or removal" actions that may constitute recalls include inspecting a device for problems, repairing a device, notifying patients of a problem with their device, relabeling a device, adjusting settings on a device, monitoring patients for health issues, etc.[28] The FDA's recall database provides

---

24. See https://www.fda.gov/advisory-committees/medical-devices/medical-devices-advisory -committee.

25. Data downloaded on March 2, 2022, from https://www.fda.gov/medical-devices/mandatory -reporting-requirements-manufacturers-importers-and-device-user-facilities/manufacturer -and-user-facility-device-experience-database-maude.

26. Manually downloaded and scraped recall database from FDA in May 2021 from https:// www.accessdata.fda.gov/scripts/cdrh/cfdocs/cfres/res.cfm.

27. See https://www.fda.gov/medical-devices/mandatory-reporting-requirements -manufacturers-importers-and-device-user-facilities/about-manufacturer-and-user-facility -device-experience-maude.

28. See https://www.fda.gov/medical-devices/medical-device-recalls/what-medical-device -recall.

detailed information on the date and severity of a recall. The FDA clearly defines three classes of medical device recalls:

- **Class I**: A situation where there is a reasonable chance that a product will cause serious health problems or death
- **Class II**: A situation where a product may cause a temporary or reversible health problem or where there is a slight chance that it will cause serious health problems or death
- **Class III**: A situation where a product is not likely to cause any health problem or injury

The FDA's recall database was manually downloaded and scraped, such that all medical device recalls are linked to their associated product(s) via its 510(k) number. This allows recalls and specific products to be directly linked.[29] Similarly, the MAUDE database includes a flag for the 510(k) number of the device associated with each adverse event report, allowing each adverse event to be linked to its respective product.

The next steps use text analysis to identify devices with a software component as well as those that incorporate AI (AI devices as defined above.) Both exercises rely on the availability of machine-readable, publicly available summary documents (as described in section 4.2.1). Among the 30,779 top-eight specialty devices cleared during our period of analysis, 30,294 (or 98.4 percent) had such documents available, and these form the basis of the text analysis used to flag those of interest. We apply the algorithm described in Foroughi and Stern (2019) to identify all software devices (both SiMD and SaMD) and then perform a further keyword search to identify AI devices as a subset of those. The keywords specifically selected for this exercise are "artificial intelligence," "deep learning," "machine learning," and "neural network." These terms were chosen for their direct relationship with the description of AI algorithms and their likely lack of ambiguity when used as such.[30] Manual inspection of a random sample of device summaries confirmed a 0 percent rate of false positives based on this method. Figure 4.1 presents a flow chart of how the analysis sample was constructed, and table 4.2 presents a breakdown of the analysis sample by medical specialty.

---

29. The databases are merged in a "many-to-one" fashion, since an individual recall event can potentially impact more than one medical device. For example, a recall due to a safety issue with a material that is used in multiple devices would impact all devices that contain that material. Similarly, a recall impacting a piece of medical device software would impact all devices that run that software.

30. An initial version of the keyword list included the word "algorithm." However, manual review suggested that it was being used in several cases where the device was collecting data that could be fed into an analysis program or used in a decision algorithm, where the product or method in question was not an AI tool. As such, the more conservative version of our keyword-based identification of AI devices does not incorporate the word "algorithm," but we continue to count its use among otherwise-identified AI devices, noting that there are virtually no "false positive" uses of the word conditional on it being used in the context of a product with other AI-related keywords in its description. For an excellent summary of deep learning techniques such as neural networks, see Hinton (2018).

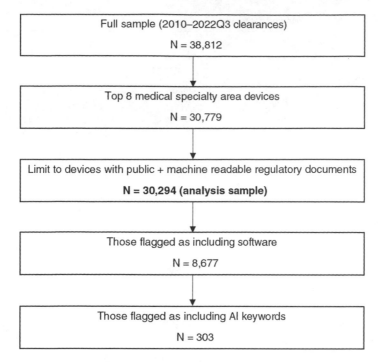

Fig. 4.1   Analysis sample construction

Table 4.2   **Analysis sample devices by specialty**

Specialty (FDA Advisory Committee Panels)	Analysis sample	All software	All AI software
Clinical chemistry and clinical toxicology	1,408 (4.7%)	375 (4.3%)	1 (0.3%)
Cardiovascular	4,355 (14.4%)	1,515 (17.5%)	14 (4.6%)
Dental	2,928 (9.7%)	466 (5.4%)	0 (0.0%)
Gastroenterology-urology	1,979 (6.5%)	428 (4.9%)	4 (1.3%)
General hospital and personal use	3,796 (12.5%)	462 (5.3%)	0 (0.0%)
Orthopedic and rehabilitation	6,893 (22.8%)	471 (5.4%)	0 (0.0%)
Radiology	4,752 (15.7%)	3,729 (43.0%)	283 (93.4%)
General and plastic surgery	4,183 (13.8%)	1,231 (14.2%)	1 (0.33%)
Total	**30,294 (100.0%)**	**8,677 (100.0%)**	**303 (100.0%)**

A few interesting findings emerge from reviewing summary statistics from the analysis sample (table 4.3). First, it is notable that nearly 29 percent of the analysis sample devices included software. This is consistent with Foroughi and Stern (2019), who document significant digitization of the medical device industry with the highest rates of SiMD and SaMD seen in radiology devices, followed by cardiology devices. Having a digitized device that includes a software component is, of course, a necessary but not sufficient condition for the incorporation of AI.

Table 4.3   Summary statistics

	Analysis sample	All software	All AI software
Keyword-based flags (all binary)			
software	8,677 (28.6%)	8,677 (100.0%)	303 (100%)
algorithm	1,884 (6.2%)	1,724 (19.9%)	256 (85%)
artificial intelligence	118 (0.4%)	118 (1.4%)	118 (39%)
deep learning	132 (0.4%)	132 (1.5%)	132 (44%)
machine learning	122 (0.4%)	122 (1.4%)	122 (40%)
neural network	90 (0.3%)	90 (1.0%)	90 (30)
Device features (binary)			
Breakthrough Device Program	9 (0.03%)	4 (0.05%)	2 (0.7%)
De Novo	128 (0.4%)	83 (1.0%)	5 (1.7%)
Firm information			
US-based application	66.3%	57.7%	46.5%
Publicly listed	30.7%	39.1%	39.3%
Revenue in $ millions if public, mean	23,955	35,467	51,924
Employees if public, mean	75,013	118,476	163,436
R&D spend if public, mean	1,633	2,083	3,219
Total number of devices	**30,294**	**8,677**	**303**

While the sample sizes are small, table 4.3 also indicates that software devices and AI devices appear more likely to have received the Breakthrough Device Designation: while just 0.03 percent of all analysis sample devices received this designation, the rate rises to 0.05 percent among software devices and 0.7 percent among AI devices. The use of the De Novo pathway is also nearly two times more common among AI devices, a fact that is consistent with these devices being more likely to be novel and less likely to have a clear "predicate" product, although these summary statistics too are based on relatively small totals. Perhaps most interestingly, we note a significant difference in the likelihood that the manufacturer of a software or AI device is a publicly listed firm: the share of all AI devices brought to market by public firms is 39.3 percent, versus 39.1 percent for software devices and 30.7 percent for all sample devices. That is, over 60 percent of AI and software devices (versus roughly 70 percent of comparator devices from the same specialties) are being brought to market by privately held firms. This indicates that digital devices are being developed by a differentiated group of innovator firms, which may in turn have different needs and backgrounds.

Figure 4.2 shows the growth in both software devices as well as AI devices over the sample period. Consistent with past work (Foroughi and Stern 2019), we observe significant, continued growth in software devices (left axis), with the number of new devices cleared per year more than doubling over the period of observation. AI device growth (right axis) shows even

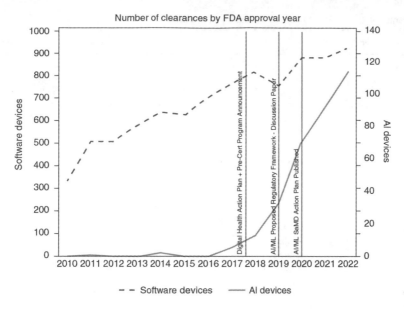

Fig. 4.2   Growth in software and AI devices

more dramatic growth (albeit off a much lower base), with annual clearances of no more than just a few devices per year through 2016 and then rising dramatically to 91 in just the first three quarters of 2021. (NB: in figure 4.2, the totals for the data point used for 2022 were inflated by a factor of 4/3 to generate an annualized number.)

Because the 510(k) database includes a field for the applicant firm's addresses, we can also report on the address from which each application was submitted (NB: this is the address from which the firm submitted the application, not necessarily the same as the address of the headquarter of the manufacturer firm. However, in many cases, this may be a more accurate representation of where R&D took place. For example, a German medical device firm that has its software development team/division in the United States might submit an application from the address of that US division.) Table 4.4 reveals that AI devices are more likely to come from international applicants than either comparator group in the analysis sample. Overall, 66.3 percent of all sample devices submitted regulatory applications from a US address, relative to 57.7 percent of software devices and just 46.5 percent of AI devices. A natural question to ask is which other countries are developing AI devices. Table 4.4 presents the distribution of the nationalities of AI device submissions. Notably, while the United States is the most represented country in the sample, US applications represent less than half (46.5 percent) of the AI products identified, highlighting the importance of

Table 4.4   AI devices by country of application

Country code	Country	Count	Percentage of AI sample
US	United States	141	46.53
IL	Israel	33	10.89
JP	Japan	26	8.58
FR	France	15	4.95
CN	China	13	4.29
KR	South Korea	12	3.96
NL	Netherlands	10	3.3
SE	Sweden	7	2.31
CA	Canada	6	1.98
DE	Germany	6	1.98
GB	United Kingdom	6	1.98
AU	Australia	5	1.65
TW	Taiwan	5	1.65
FI	Finland	3	0.99
IN	India	3	0.99
SG	Singapore	3	0.99
BE	Belgium	2	0.66
IE	Ireland	2	0.66
AT	Austria	1	0.33
BG	Bulgaria	1	0.33
DK	Denmark	1	0.33
PT	Portugal	1	0.33
VN	Vietnam	1	0.33
Total		303	100

other countries such as Israel, Japan, France, and China in the AI device development ecosystem.

A final set of descriptive statistics explores the safety profiles of our sample devices. As described above, we consider both adverse events and recalls as relevant safety outcomes. We consider the first two years after a product is cleared for marketing in order to capture the most relevant period of time after a new product's launch and to ensure that adverse event and recall outcomes are comparable across older versus newer devices.

Panel I of table 4.5 presents outcomes for the entire dataset (which is truncated due to the inability to observe two years of follow-up data for those devices approved during or after 2020 Q3). Panel II includes only safety outcomes for devices cleared through 2020 (but includes outcome data through 2022 Q3) for a subsample with a balanced follow-up period. The obvious tradeoff in building the balanced subsample is the quantity of data: since over half of AI devices in the sample were cleared in 2021 and 2022, the total number of AI devices considered (right-most column) drops significantly from Panel I to Panel II.

The safety outcome data reveal an interesting story: adverse events appear

Table 4.5   **Device safety outcomes**

Panel I: Safety outcomes (all years)	Analysis sample	All software	All AI software
Adverse events (AE)			
Any AE in the first two years	4,212 (13.9%)	1,047 (12.1%)	9 (3.0%)
Any mandatory AE report in the first two years	4,206 (13.9%)	1,044 (12.0%)	9 (3.0%)
Average # of AEs in the first two years (count)	15.861	46.250	0.046
Average # of mandatory AEs in the first two years (count)	15.855	46.244	0.046
Recalls			
Any recall in the first two years	1,158 (3.8%)	523 (6.0%)	5 (1.7%)
. . . categorized as Class I	39 (0.1%)	14 (0.2%)	0 (0.0%)
. . . categorized as Class II	1,103 (3.6%)	509 (5.9%)	5 (1.7%)
. . . categorized as Class III	29 (0.1%)	4 (0.1%)	0 (0.0%)
Average # recalls in the first two years (count)	0.052	0.092	0.046
. . . categorized as Class I	0.001	0.002	0.000
. . . categorized as Class II	0.050	0.090	0.046
. . . categorized as Class III	0.001	0.000	0.000
Total number of devices	**30,294 (100.0%)**	**8,677 (100.0%)**	**303 (100.0%)**
Panel II: Safety outcomes (2010–2020 clearances only)	Analysis sample	All software	All AI software
Adverse events (AE)			
Any AE in the first two years	4,121 (15.9%)	1,011 (14.2%)	9 (7.1%)
Any mandatory AE report in the first two years	4,115 (15.9%)	1,008 (14.2%)	9 (7.1%)
Average # of AEs in the first two years (count)	18.454	56.388	0.111
Average # of mandatory AEs in the first two years (count)	18.447	56.381	0.111
Recalls			
Any recall in the first two years	1,154 (4.4%)	519 (7.3%)	5 (4.0%)
. . . categorized as Class I	39 (0.1%)	14 (0.2%)	0 (0.0%)
. . . categorized as Class II	1,099 (4.2%)	505 (7.1%)	5 (4.0%)
. . . categorized as Class III	29 (0.1%)	4 (0.1%)	0 (0.0%)
Average # Recalls in the first two years (count)	0.061	0.112	0.111
. . . categorized as Class I	0.002	0.002	0.000
. . . categorized as Class II	0.058	0.109	0.111
. . . categorized as Class III	0.001	0.001	0.000
Total number of devices	**25,962 (100.0%)**	**7,108 (100.0%)**	**126 (100.0%)**

similarly likely to be recorded when comparing software devices to the full sample of devices; however, the likelihood of an AI device having any adverse event reports drops dramatically in both samples. When considering *counts* of adverse events, both samples suggest a roughly 3x increase in adverse events among software devices relative to the overall sample, but a more than 100x decrease in adverse event counts per device among AI devices, again hinting at their relative safety.

Similarly, data on recalls (a thankfully much rarer outcome) suggest that software devices are more likely to experience recalls (and when they do, they experience more of them) relative to the full sample; however, AI devices are either modestly or significantly less likely to experience recalls. While more work is needed to understand the drivers of adverse event reports and medical device recalls, the findings here paint a preliminarily sanguine picture of AI device safety: on average, AI devices appear to be at least as good as or better than comparable samples of devices in terms of the likelihoods with which negative safety outcomes are observed. These findings are consistent with Everhart and Stern (forthcoming), who find somewhat higher rates of adverse events and recalls among software devices in many settings; however, these results suggest an added layer of nuance in that the subset of AI-driven devices identified here are actually less likely to experience adverse safety-related outcomes.

4.3   Innovation Incentives

How should innovation policy researchers think about the intersection of medical AI and medical product regulation, and what can be learned from early data on regulated AI in the United States? A clear starting point for answering the first questions is the FDA's current position on the regulation of AI/ML products, which was articulated in early 2021 in the *Artificial Intelligence and Machine Learning (AI/ML) Software as a Medical Device Action Plan* published by the CDRH's Digital Health Center of Excellence (US FDA 2021) and the *Proposed Regulatory Framework for Modifications to Artificial Intelligence/Machine Learning (AI/ML)-Based Software as a Medical Device (SaMD)—Discussion Paper and Request for Feedback* published previously (US FDA 2019). Ideas in both documents rely on the risk categorization principles outlined by the IMDRF[31] and are based on the "total lifecycle approach" envisioned by the software Pre-Cert pilot program.

A key part of the proposed framework for the future regulation of AI/ML devices is the "algorithm change protocol," which would rely on real-world performance data and ongoing monitoring to allow regulators to flexibly balance the FDA's dual mandate to protect public health while still providing timely access to new products. More generally, the action plan outlines five key actions that it sees as the focus of FDA's work going forward:

1. Tailored regulatory framework for AI/ML-based SaMD
2. FDA to encourage harmonization of good machine learning practice (GMLP) development (an analog to GMP in physical devices)
3. Patient-centered approach incorporating transparency to users

---

31. See https://www.fda.gov/medical-devices/software-medical-device-samd/global-approach-software-medical-device.

4. Regulatory science methods related to algorithm bias and robustness
5. Real-world performance

The fact that the action plan exists and that its first articulated goal is the establishment of a tailored regulatory framework for AI/ML-based SaMD send a clear signal that US regulators are aware of the special challenges (and opportunities) inherent in the regulation of AI-based SaMD. And yet great uncertainty remains as to how precisely AI device regulation will be implemented in practice—and, as is always the case—the devil will be in the details. As just one example, understanding whether casual inference will play a role in the FDA's regulation of certain types of products will meaningfully shape the types of products brought to market—both within the regulated setting and beyond (Stern and Price 2020).

A laundry list of other questions that flow from the action plan's component sections remain unanswered: For example, what will be the scope and specificity of the tailored regulatory framework that emerges? The CDRH plans to encourage the harmonization[32] of GMLPs, which are expected to include best practices for data management, feature extraction, training, interpretability, evaluation, and documentation that FDA acknowledges as being "akin to good software engineering practices or quality system practices" (US FDA 2021)—how detailed and how burdensome (two related but ultimately distinct features) will these GMLPs be? How closely aligned will they be with the state-of-the-art in algorithm development? The answers to both questions—in particular, the latter—will meaningfully shape the barriers to entry for developers to enter the regulated SaMD space.

In addition to active participation in the IMDRF's AI Medical Device Working Group, the FDA maintains relationships with the Institute of Electrical and Electronics Engineers' AI medical device working group as well as the International Organization for Standardization/Joint Technical Committee's Sub-Committee on AI and the British Standards Institution's initiative on AI in medical technology (US FDA 2021).[33] Such relationships are deeply important: (internationally recognized) standard-setting organizations are known to be vital for identifying the most promising technologies and influencing the trajectory of technology adoption in other contexts (Rysman and Simcoe 2008), and regulatory clarity is known to accelerate time-to-market for other types of medical devices (Stern 2017).

With respect to patient-centricity in incorporating transparency for users, regulatory science methods related to algorithm bias and robustness, and the creative, but still-rigorous application of real-world performance data,

32. The FDA is also moving to harmonize regulatory guidelines with international standards for quality systems such as ISO 13485, which covers quality management systems for medical devices and requirements for regulatory purposes (https://www.iso.org/standard/59752.html).
33. In 2021, the FDA officially joined the Xavier AI World Consortium Collaborative Community and the Pathology Innovation Collaborative Community, and also participates in the Collaborative Community on Ophthalmic Imaging (US FDA 2021)

countless questions of a similar nature remain to be articulated by stake-holders and answered by regulators. The ways neural networks and other AI/ML algorithms perform tasks present a particular challenge for regulators; at present, complete transparency remains out of reach (Hinton 2018). Nonetheless, there needs to be a mechanism to build trust in the outcomes via specific validation tests, which is where real-world performance studies can play an important role. On all of these topics, the broader digital medicine community can also collaborate to move medical AI forward; for example, in articulating best practices and priorities for the generation and using of real-world evidence in the assessment of digital health products (Stern et al. 2022). This work will necessarily touch on patient-centricity, transparency, and various aspects of regulatory science. For example, the articulation of best practices for real-world evidence generation will lead to greater consensus on questions of how to handle and understand the implications of missing data, characterizing the generalizability and trans-portability of findings to broad populations, and understanding and stan-dardizing hypothesis testing around whether digital health products are complements or substitutes to existing standards of care, to name just a few aspects. Finally, other questions that are not covered in the scope of the action plan also surface quickly: What about the large number of AI devices (as defined here) that are SiMD, rather than SaMD products? The scope of the action plan is explicitly limited to stand-alone software, with the corollary that a good deal of uncertainty may remain for AI SiMD products.

Against this backdrop, innovation policy questions associated with the concept of *regulatory uncertainty* become all the more trenchant: in the US medical device setting, regulatory uncertainty—e.g., as experienced when a first-of-its-kind medical device goes through a regulatory approval process for the first time—has been associated with first-mover disadvantages and lower rates of novel device commercialization among small firms (Stern 2017). There is every reason to believe that regulatory uncertainty will nega-tively impact firms' willingness to engage in innovation in the regulated space broadly and to embark on more novel R&D projects (specifically, those without regulatory precedent) in particular. But this also indicates the great potential that proactive approaches could have in this setting: the provision of regulatory clarity through formal guidance documents has been shown to speed regulatory approval of new high-risk devices (Stern 2017), suggesting the vital role that regulatory innovation and policy clarification can play in shaping innovation incentives.

The value of regulatory innovation and regulatory clarity may be particu-larly important in the context of AI devices because such a large share of innovations to date have emerged from smaller firms and those from other countries. Large (e.g., publicly listed) and domestic firms are far more likely to possess US regulatory expertise in the first place, and these firms also have, on average, more experience in the (US) regulated product space than their smaller and/or internationally based peers. Yet evidence from the early years of AI device rollout in the United States suggests that privately held international manufacturers are disproportionately likely to be developing AI devices relative to what is otherwise seen in the regulated space.

Taking an even larger step back, it is worth considering the margin between regulated and unregulated AI tools—that is, asking the "extensive margin question": What role does regulation *itself* play in innovation incentives for new AI devices? As is often the case, the answer is "It depends": in some situations—for example, to get a product to market more quickly—pursuing a nonregulated product development approach may be incentivized. In other cases, however, having a *regulated* product on the market may itself be part of the commercialization and/or reimbursement strategy for a digital tool.

The gray area in which many devices reside and in which many manufacturers operate is substantial, and there may be strategic reasons to pursue FDA regulation or to avoid it. One reason to pursue a strategy of formal regulation is that reimbursement by payers may be more straightforward for regulated medical products, increasing manufacturers' appetite for going through a clearance process, since it may be a significant component of their reimbursement strategy. In the extreme, this is already being seen in the case of "prescription digital therapeutics" (sometimes called PDTs), which are software-based (SaMD) therapeutic devices that are intended only for prescription by clinicians. Notably, the label PDT is one that was created by the SaMD industry. Unlike with drugs, the word *prescription* does not (necessarily) indicate anything about the product's risk level; rather, the term is often used as part of a market access strategy for the manufacturer, which in turn is making a bet that products prescribed by physicians will be more likely to qualify for insurance coverage than direct-to-consumer apps/tools. Indeed, anecdotes suggest that other types of digital health companies are pursuing an FDA regulatory pathway in order to gain legitimacy in the eyes of clinician recommenders and health insurance companies. Such behavior has precedent: Eisenberg (2019) describes how a situation of "opting into device regulation" has been observed among developers of next generation sequencing diagnostic tests for tumor DNA, where "understanding the rules and practices that govern health insurance coverage and the important role of FDA in assessment of new technologies" is key to understanding such a decision by a manufacturer.

On the other hand, manufacturers may deliberately select language so as to *avoid* making medical claims that would require premarket review in order to get products to market faster or at a lower cost, since FDA submissions are notoriously costly to file and take several months to years. Relatedly, many SaMD products will meet the definition of a medical device, but qualify for enforcement discretion (e.g., because they pose only a very low risk to patients), such that they are, de facto, not regulated by the FDA. A final set of innovations are likely to emerge outside of the regulated space, but may have spillover effects on the types of other AI products that can be commercialized. For example, Price, Sachs, and Eisenberg (2021) point out that AI tools such as those that might be used for quality improvement initiatives or for optimizing use of scarce hospital facilities are likely to be developed by health systems and insurers (rather than machine learning experts and/or medical device companies), since these parties already control the relevant training datasets and have the greatest operational interest in such products' development. Importantly, the authors note, "data possession and control play a larger role in determining capacity to innovate in this [more operationally oriented] space" (Price, Sachs, and Eisenberg 2021). In certain cases, of course, there will not be any gray area: very high- (or very low-) risk products will (or will not) unambiguously qualify as regulated medical devices, and these realities, in turn, could impact the availability of datasets for AI development in other settings.

Notably, the FDA does not actively regulate two significant types of AI systems that are likely to play a growing role in care delivery as well as in AI R&D (Stern and Price 2020). First, the FDA does not regulate certain types of clinical decision support software (CDS), software that "helps providers make care decisions by, for instance, providing suggested drug dosages or alerts about drug interactions." When providers have an opportunity to review the rationale behind the recommendation made by an AI, it is likely to be exempt from what FDA considers a device (21 US Code § 360j). However recent regulatory guidance has served to significantly narrow the set of applications that qualify as CDS,[34] and as a corollary, many more applications are likely to be considered devices. Further, some AI tools will be considered "laboratory-developed tests," which are those that are developed and used within a single healthcare facility such as a hospital. For such tests, the FDA also holds back from exercising its regulatory authority. In both cases, we should expect to see notable growth in AI, although use cases with cost and/or comparative effectiveness have yet to be established.

4.4   Conclusion

A survey of the regulated medical device landscape suggests a dramatic uptick in the commercialization of AI products over recent years. At the same time, regulators have begun a germane and important discussion of how such devices could be regulated constructively in the future—ultimately under the umbrella of the FDA's dual mandate of ensuring public health while facilitating patient access to important new medical technologies. There are several margins along which innovation incentives are likely to play a role. To the extent that many applications of AI for diagnosis and treatment of medical conditions are likely to meet the formal definition of

---

34. See https://www.fda.gov/media/109618/download.

a medical device, medical product regulation will be an ongoing presence in this space—and one that will shape incentives for software developers, established medical device companies, venture capital investors, and user-innovators.

Whether an AI tool qualifies as a medical device and the extent to which the answer occupies the gray area of ambiguity on this question will impact whether products are developed, which R&D decisions are made at the margin, and how new AI tools are paid for in the healthcare system once they are commercialized. Among regulated devices, meaningful differences in the burden of clinical evidence and paperwork required for commercialization already exist, depending on whether a device is classified as being of low, moderate, or high risk. These differences will be even more salient for AI developers, who are likely to have less medical device regulatory experience than those engaging in R&D activities in traditional medical technology firms. And of course, emergent guidelines from the FDA and best practices from the broader digital medicine community (including clinical researchers, standard-setting organizations, and companies) will impact the amount of uncertainty associated with new product development in this space and therefore the incentives for firms—both small and large—to innovate.

Such guidelines and best practices will of course emerge in the context of a larger societal conversation about AI in healthcare and must *necessarily* be considered against the backdrop of key issues such as those highlighted by the US National Academy of Medicine (Matheny et al. 2019). These include the imperative of promoting population-representative data with accessibility, standardization, and quality; prioritizing ethical, equitable, and inclusive healthcare AI while addressing explicit and implicit bias; contextualizing the dialogue of transparency and trust according to differential needs; cultivating a near-term focus on augmented intelligence versus AI autonomous agents; developing and deploying appropriate training and educational programs; leveraging frameworks and best practices for learning healthcare systems, human factors, and implementation science; and balancing innovation with safety via regulation and legislation to promote trust (Matheny, Israni, and Whicher 2020)—a final priority that brings the discussion back to the role of regulatory and legal aspects of medical AI.

The emergence of regulated AI devices holds great promise for delivering higher-quality care to patients and addressing unserved or underserved populations. It also can improve workflows, efficiency, and confidence in diagnosis and treatment decisions for clinicians, with secondary benefits to healthcare payers and clear financial benefits to product companies. Yet ongoing regulatory clarity and policy innovation efforts will be necessary for regulation to keep pace with AI innovation in healthcare. Further research on innovation policy in medical AI should focus on understanding which aspects of regulatory clarity and regulatory policy are most likely to induce and facilitate the commercialization of welfare-enhancing innovations.

References

Alon, Noy, Ariel Dora Stern, and John Torous. 2020. "Assessing the Food and Drug Administration's Risk-Based Framework for Software Precertification with Top Health Apps in the United States: Quality Improvement Study." *JMIR mHealth and uHealth* 8 (10): e20482.

Benjamens, Stan, Pranavsingh Dhunnoo, and Bertalan Meskó. 2020. "The State of Artificial Intelligence-Based FDA-Approved Medical Devices and Algorithms: An Online Database." *NPJ Digital Medicine* 3 (1): 1–8.

Brönneke, Jan Benedikt, Jennifer Müller, Konstantinos Mouratis, Julia Hagen, and Ariel Dora Stern. 2021. "Regulatory, Legal, and Market Aspects of Smart Wearables for Cardiac Monitoring." *Sensors* 21 (14): 4937.

Eisenberg, Rebecca S. 2019. "Opting into Device Regulation in the Face of Uncertain Patentability." *Marquette Intellectual Property Law Review* 23: 1.

Everhart, Alexander O., and Ariel D. Stern. Forthcoming "Post-Market Surveillance of Software Medical Devices: Evidence from Regulatory Data." In *Diagnosing in the Home: The Ethical, Legal, and Regulatory Challenges and Opportunities of Digital Home Health*, Cambridge University Press.

Felber, Sarith, and Dawid Maciorowski. 2023. "Technology Primers: Smart Wearables and Health." Working paper, Belfer Center for Science and International Affairs, Harvard Kennedy School, Spring.

Foroughi, Cirrus, and Ariel Dora Stern. 2019. "Who Drives Digital Innovation? Evidence from the US Medical Device Industry." Harvard Business School Working Paper No. 19-120.

Hinton, Geoffrey. 2018. "Deep Learning—A Technology with the Potential to Transform Health Care." *JAMA* 320 (11): 1101–2.

IMDRF (International Medical Device Regulators Forum). 2013. *Software as a Medical Device (SaMD): Key Definitions.* IMDRF SaMD Working Group.

Matheny, Michael, S. Thadaney Israni, Mahnoor Ahmed, and Danielle Whicher. 2019. *Artificial Intelligence in Healthcare: The Hope, the Hype, the Promise, the Peril.* Washington, DC: National Academy of Medicine.

Matheny, Michael E., Danielle Whicher, and Sonoo Thadaney Israni. 2020. "Artificial Intelligence in Healthcare: A Report from the National Academy of Medicine." *JAMA* 323 (6): 509–10.

Price, W., I. I. Nicholson, Rachel E. Sachs, and Rebecca S. Eisenberg. 2021. "New Innovation Models in Medical AI." *Washington University Law Review* 99 (4): 1121.

Rysman, Marc, and Timothy Simcoe. 2008. "Patents and the Performance of Voluntary Standard-Setting Organizations." *Management Science* 54 (11): 1920–34.

Sanders, Samantha F., Mats Terwiesch, William J. Gordon, and Ariel D. Stern. 2019. "How Artificial Intelligence Is Changing Health Care Delivery." *NEJM Catalyst* 5 (5).

Stern, Ariel Dora. 2017. "Innovation under Regulatory Uncertainty: Evidence from Medical Technology." *Journal of Public Economics* 145: 181–200.

Stern, Ariel D., Jan Brönneke, Jörg F. Debatin, Julia Hagen, Henrik Matthies, Smit Patel, Ieuan Clay, Bjoern Eskofier, Annika Herr, Kurt Hoeller, Ashley Jaksa, Daniel B. Kramer, Mattias Kyhlstedt, Katherine T. Lofgren, Nirosha Mahendraratnam, Holger Muehlan, Simon Reif, Lars Riedemann, and Jennifer C. Goldsack. 2022. "Advancing Digital Health Applications: Priorities for Innovation in Real-World Evidence Generation." *Lancet Digital Health* 4 (3): e200–e206.

Stern, Ariel Dora, and W. Nicholson Price. 2020. "Regulatory Oversight, Causal Inference, and Safe and Effective Health Care Machine Learning." *Biostatistics* 21 (2): 363–67.

Torous, John, Ariel D. Stern, and Florence T. Bourgeois. 2022. "Regulatory Consid-
    erations to Keep Pace with Innovation in Digital Health Products." *NPJ Digital
    Medicine* 5 (1): 1–4.
US FDA (Food and Drug Administration). 2019. *Proposed Regulatory Framework
    for Modifications to Artificial Intelligence/Machine Learning (AI/ML)-Based Soft-
    ware as a Medical Device (SaMD)—Discussion Paper and Request for Feedback.*
    Digital Health Center of Excellence, CDRH.
US FDA (Food and Drug Administration). 2021. *Artificial Intelligence and Machine
    Learning (AI/ML) Software as a Medical Device Action Plan.* Digital Health
    Center of Excellence, CDRH.

Comment   Boris Babic

Introduction

In the development of medical artificial intelligence (medical AI) applications there exists a pressing set of open questions around how to effectively
build the associated regulatory landscape. Among these questions is what
the role of the US Food and Drug Administration (FDA) and its counter-
parts in other countries should be, and how much we should now rely on the
institutional infrastructure that historically evolved for the oversight of traditional (non-AI) software in medical devices. In "The Regulation of Medical AI: Policy Approaches, Data, and Innovation Incentives," Stern develops
a very illuminating project that can help us begin to chart answers to these
questions. The project is backed by an insightful empirical analysis—using
FDA data on cleared medical AI devices together with data on adverse
events and recalls—that sheds further light on who is developing these technologies, how they are performing, and their relative safety.

In this comment I will offer (1) a partial summary of Stern's article, (2) a
brief analysis of the interesting empirical insights, and (3) a more open-
textured discussion of the emerging trends and unsettled questions in medical AI regulation.

Partial Summary

While there is a large variety of medical AI applications, as Stern explains,
substantial energy and attention centers on those that are performing or
assisting in diagnostic and treatment tasks. These are likely to qualify as

Boris Babic is an assistant professor of statistical sciences and of philosophy at the University
of Toronto.

For acknowledgments, sources of research support, and disclosure of the author's material
financial relationships, if any, please see https://www.nber.org/books-and-chapters/economics
-artificial-intelligence-health-care-challenges/comment-regulation-medical-ai-policy
-approaches-data-and-innovation-incentives-babic.

medical devices under the 1976 Medical Device Amendment to the 1938 Federal Food, Drug, and Cosmetic Act. The 1938 act is the chief statute empowering the FDA with authority to oversee the safety of medical products.

When a technology qualifies as a medical device, the FDA takes a tripartite approach to its regulation. The lowest-risk (Class I) devices are subject only to modest (manufacturing) controls. Moderate-risk (Class II) devices are regulated through a process called Premarket Notification (or the 510(k) Pathway), requiring the maker to demonstrate either substantial equivalence to an existing regulated device or to pass a De Novo classification request. The De Novo process in turn requires the maker to provide reasonable assurance of safety and effectiveness of the device for its intended use. Finally, the highest-risk (Class III) devices require Premarket Approval, which typically includes evidence from clinical trials.

When it comes to medical AI, most devices are dubbed software as a medical device (SaMD) by the FDA—as opposed to software in a medical device (SiMD)—and are going through the moderate-risk (Class II) processes. For example, Benjamens, Dhunnoo, and Bertalan (2020) compiled a database of medical AI technologies that have been cleared by the FDA, and of the 79 devices on their list, all but two were brought to market under the Category II scheme—i.e., going through the 510(k) or De Novo pathway.

Accordingly, Stern's empirical analysis runs through the following pipeline: Stern begins with the full FDA 510(k) database for the years 2010–2022 Q3, containing over 38,000 devices. The scope is then further limited to applications in eight of the largest medical specialties, resulting in approximately 31,000 clearances. This database is then merged with two additional sources of information: data from the FDA's medical device adverse event reporting database and data from the FDA's recall database. Stern then uses text analysis to identify devices with a software component (~8,500 devices), and among those Stern uses additional keywords to identify AI-based software devices as a proper subset (303 devices). Importantly, the keywords used to identify AI based devices are "artificial intelligence," "deep learning," "machine learning," and "neural network."

Empirical Insights

Some interesting trends worth highlighting are the following: the use of the Class II De Novo pathway is twice as common among AI devices, the majority of devices are being brought to market by privately held firms, and the number of clearances has more than doubled per year during the observation period. Globally, the United States, Israel, and Japan hold a disproportionate share of the medical AI innovation market. While it is small surprise that the United States has the most FDA clearances, the outsize performance of Israel and Japan relative to its peer countries with strong biomedical innovation, such as France and South Korea, is interesting.

Perhaps the most notable, however, is Stern's analysis of device safety outcomes—made possible by the merging of 510(k) clearance data with data on adverse event reports and recalls. While it is very insightful, it is also necessarily preliminary—because we simply do not have enough devices or a long enough observation period to make more definitive statements about the relative safety of medical AI versus non-AI technologies.

For example, in the full sample of approximately 30,000 devices, there were slightly over 4,000 adverse event reports. For the subset of devices containing software (AI or non-AI) there were just over 1,000 adverse event reports, out of a total of approximately 8,500 devices. And for AI-based medical devices, there were 9 adverse event reports out of a total of approximately 300 devices. Meanwhile, for recalls, there are 1,000 recalls in the full sample, just over 500 in the subset of software based devices, and 5 in the subset of AI based software devices. While this suggests that, proportionately, medical AI devices are overall safer, we must temper that conclusion by how much we can learn from the small numbers observed over a relatively short period. As an aside, assessments of adverse event reports also have a censoring problem worth taking into consideration—we cannot distinguish between the nonoccurrence of an event and an event that occurred but was unreported.

There is also an interesting methodological question here. Consider a hypothetical example: In medical materials engineering, emerging technologies are often quite invasive—such as catheters, ventricular assist devices, and heart stents. They are used to treat very serious illness, and their role in the body can be critical to a patient's survival. As a result, the potential for things to go wrong is substantial. And when things do go wrong, they go wrong unambiguously—for example, a device breaks in the patient's body or stops pumping blood as it should. This is not an ideal example, because such devices would likely be Class III devices, but I use it here merely to illustrate a general point: in nonmedical AI devices used for treatment, it is clear how defects can occur and it is likewise clear what would constitute evidence of such defects.

But now consider some archetypal medical AI applications. For example, consider an imaging diagnostic assistant tool—a device that, say, reads an x-ray and outputs a probability of a bone fracture. What would be a mistake or a malfunction in this case? After all, the result is produced in the form of a probability. And it is used in conjunction with a radiologist's expert opinion. So unless the device crashes, it is hard to envision a situation where we would see evidence of a defect from its performance.

One thing we might do is try to stress test the device in an adversarial fashion—try to identify cases where small changes in input lead to large changes in output, as Babic et al. (2019) suggest. This would be closer to a defect, because the classification function is failing to satisfy a Lipschitz condition, so to speak—cases that are similar along some metric in their inputs are treated very differently in their outputs. But this is not something that users would do in the ordinary application of medical AI devices. And that further suggests that in the world of medical AI, perhaps we will need to focus more on ongoing regulation and assessment, as Gerke et al. (2020) argue, than on traditional adverse event reports or user-identified problems leading to recalls.

Emerging Trends and Open Questions

This leads to the final section. I will focus on three open questions: updating, model transparency, and regulatory loopholes.

Updating

The above considerations suggest that traditional approaches to evaluating safety performance may not be ideal as applied to medical AI devices. This is consistent with what Babic et al. (2019) dub the "update problem." Traditionally, the FDA has required software-based medical devices to undergo a new round of review every time the underlying code is changed.

As Stern explains, for a Class II device, there are no regulatory provisions for amending or changing an existing 510(k) clearance, and any modification would presumably require a new 510(k) to be submitted. Class III devices require a "PMA supplement," an onerous submission justifying the software changes. In other words, once a SaMD is approved, the associated software is locked on approval.

This makes for a very unproductive regulatory approach for medical AI, where the main benefit comes from the algorithm's ability to learn from new data. For instance, imagine a simple linear classification function where the odds of x are given by $e^{\beta_0 \beta_x'}$. As part of the approval process the β parameter coefficients would be fit to some training sample. Now, as the algorithm is applied in practice and new observations come in, would a change in the βs trigger a requirement for a new 510(k)? Plausibly yes, because any change in the βs can change the input-output relationship, which the FDA requires to be fixed. Such a policy is very antithetical to the "learning" in machine learning.

As Stern recognizes, the FDA has recently proposed a new total product life-cycle regulatory approach, which would move away from the black-and-white practice of approve/deny and its associated discouragement of software updates. Since this proposal is still in its infancy, it is hard to know how it will look, but in principle it could make for a more productive partnership between the FDA and medical AI manufacturers. Indeed, it could allow regulators to move away from looking at isolated adverse event reports and to take a more participatory and ongoing monitoring role of medical AI devices—to take a system view, as Gerke et al. (2020) suggest. For example, regulators can be on the lookout for common modeling problems that can lead to patient harm, such as concept drift, covariate shift, and model instability (in the sense of similar inputs leading to very different outputs) (Babic et al. 2019).

Model Transparency

Stern identifies AI devices using the keywords enumerated above—such as "deep learning" and "neural network." These keywords are typically associated with so-called black box machine learning models, and it is worth considering whether there are other medical AI applications that do not use these terms and therefore are missed by the search—for example, devices described as classification models, multivariate analyses, regressions, or statistical learning techniques. I doubt there are many, but if there are, it would be particularly illuminating to include them because such models are more likely to be transparent ("white boxes"), and a number of scholars have argued that they should be preferred in medicine (Babic et al. 2021a) and other high-stakes settings (Rudin 2019). Indeed, it would be interesting to compare the performance of different types of medical AI devices (black box versus white box) with respect to adverse event reports and recalls. It may be that white box models have less adverse event reports, but it may also be that problems are easier to identify when white box models are used, with the counterintuitive implication that they have more adverse event reports without being any less safe.

This brings up a more general question of how, if at all, model transparency should enter into the regulatory equation. Currently, the FDA is agnostic between different types of classification algorithms. That is, there is no necessary advantage to using a transparent linear model as opposed to a deep learning one, from the perspective of gaining FDA clearance for a medical AI product. But as the agency transitions to the total product life-cycle regulatory approach, it is worth considering whether the black box nature of a system's algorithm is something to be on the lookout for.

Loopholes

While significant attention has been paid to Class II and III medical AI devices, very few medical AI applications actually qualify as a device, and even if they might qualify as a device, the FDA often exercises enforcement discretion, meaning that the FDA will not enforce regulatory requirements over these products. In effect, then, they are altogether outside the scope of the FDA's regulatory purview. This is true in particular for what are deemed "health or wellness" applications (Babic et al. 2021b): for example, mobile apps that are designed to track weight and fitness levels.

Devices like these pose an interesting problem from a public policy perspective. Arguably we tolerate the manufacturers' circumventing of the regulatory landscape because the individual risk the applications pose to patients is low. For example, consider mobile phone apps that have a partial diagnostic function, such as detecting high heart rate. Since these apps tend to have high sensitivity, the biggest risk, one might think, is that of a false positive (a false health scare) requiring a specialist follow-up.

However, it is worth asking whether our regulatory infrastructure should be built around individual patient harm in the way that the regulation of medical practice is. As policy makers, we may want to look at the medical AI ecosystem as a whole. And from a social/aggregate perspective, these negligible individual costs can add up. For example, if millions of people require a specialist follow-up to correct a false positive generated by a mobile phone app, this creates a large social cost borne by taxpayers. Another way to put the point: when it comes to unregulated mobile apps, perhaps device manufacturers should be required to bear the costs of the healthcare externalities that they generate.

Concluding Remarks

At the widest level of generality, and by way of closing, it is worth asking whether we should regulate algorithms by their domain of application (medicine, criminal justice, finance, etc.), or whether we should have one agency that regulates algorithmic technologies across different domains, as Tutt (2017) has argued. Stern effectively demonstrates how the former approach, which is currently the one we take, requires agencies to significantly upgrade regulatory environments that were developed a long time ago and for very different purposes. And we see this struggle in the case of the FDA—attempting to quickly evolve their approach to governing medical software in a way that can suitably cover medical AI applications. Arguably, the latter approach (a separate agency for governing algorithms across domains) would allow for a more uniform, flexible, and holistic regulatory environment for all AI technologies, regardless of their field of application.

References

Babic, B., S. Gerke, T. Evgeniou, and I. Cohen. 2019. "Algorithms on Regulatory Lockdown in Medicine." *Science* 366 (6470): 1202–4.

Babic, B., S. Gerke, T. Evgeniou, and I. Cohen. 2021a. "Beware Explanations from AI in Health Care." *Science* 373 (6552): 284–86.

Babic, B., S. Gerke, T. Evgeniou, and I. Cohen. 2021b. "Direct-to-Consumer Medical Machine Learning and Artificial Intelligence Applications." *Nature Machine Intelligence* 3: 283–87.

Benjamens, S., P. Dhunnoo, and M. Bertalan. 2020. "The State of Artificial Intelligence-Based FDA-Approved Medical Devices and Algorithms: An Online Database." *NPJ Digital Medicine* 3 (1): 1–8.

Gerke, S., B. Babic, T. Evgeniou, and G. Cohen. 2020. "The Need for a System View to Regulate Artificial Intelligence/Machine Learning-Based Software as Medical Device." *Nature Digital Medicine* 3 (53).

Rudin, C. 2019. "Stop Explaining Black Box Machine Learning Models for High Stakes Decisions and Use Interpretable Models Instead." *Nature Machine Intelligence* 1: 206–15.

Tutt, A. 2017. "An FDA for Algorithms." *Administrative Law Review* 69 (1): 83–123.

Additional Comments

Comment on Chapters 1 and 2   Susan Feng Lu

Building Physician Trust in Artificial Intelligence

In the field of healthcare, artificial intelligence (AI) plays a pivotal role, offering two distinct functions that significantly contribute to its progress. First, AI demonstrates its exceptional ability to expedite routine tasks, thereby enhancing the efficiency of clinical operations and leading to substantial reductions in administrative costs. Notably, AI's proficiency in analyzing medical images, comparable to that of radiologists, and its seamless facilitation of medical information during patient transfers exemplify its capacity in this regard (Sahni et al. 2022). Second, AI empowers clinicians with invaluable clinical analytics, enabling them to provide comprehensive recommendations for diagnoses and treatments. A notable example includes AI's role in assisting patients in selecting appropriate physicians while simultaneously offering physicians well-informed treatment plan recommendations. Amid the brevity of this discourse, my focus shall be directed toward a specific yet burgeoning domain closely associated with the second function: the establishment of trust between physicians and AI.

To optimize the effectiveness of AI in clinical recommendations and foster a harmonious collaboration between AI systems and healthcare professionals, it is crucial to understand the intricate dynamics that unfold between AI

Susan Feng Lu is the Gerald Lyles Rising Star Professor of Management at the Mitchell E. Daniels, Jr. School of Business, Purdue University.

For acknowledgments, sources of research support, and disclosure of the author's material financial relationships, if any, please see https://www.nber.org/books-and-chapters/economics -artificial-intelligence-health-care-challenges/building-physician-trust-ai.

and physicians. In this pursuit of synergy, cultivating physician confidence in AI assumes paramount significance. The ensuing discussion delves into three key aspects that hold relevance in this matter.

The first aspect to be addressed pertains to the inherent inclination of individuals to be averse to unsolicited suggestions and to harbor negative sentiments toward opinions that diverge from their own. Within the realm of clinical operations, a multitude of applications integrating AI to generate medical recommendations are seamlessly incorporated into electronic medical record systems. Consequently, AI-generated recommendations manifest automatically on physicians' screens. However, insights derived from interviews conducted in collaboration with a renowned AI-health company illuminate that a notable proportion of physicians utilizing such systems often express annoyance toward AI-generated recommendations and seek methods to disable them. In response to these concerns, the company has implemented a feature that grants physicians the autonomy to determine whether to access AI-generated recommendations.

Background data supports the notion that the acceptance rate for AI-generated recommendations is substantially higher when physicians actively choose to enable this functionality. When physicians possess unwavering confidence in their medical judgment, AI-generated recommendations may be perceived as inconsequential or even detrimental to their expertise. However, in situations involving diagnostic or treatment complexities, where seeking a second opinion or engaging in discussions with fellow medical professionals becomes necessary, AI emerges as a valuable alternative for consultation. In such scenarios, physicians welcome AI-generated recommendations and are more inclined to accept them. Thus, affording physicians the freedom to decide whether to seek opinions from AI can significantly alleviate tension between physicians and AI, while concurrently fostering trust in AI among physicians.

The second aspect to consider revolves around the diverse range of personalities exhibited by individuals. While some individuals exhibit strong opinions, others tend to be more agreeable in nature. Recognizing and adapting to these different personality types can profoundly enhance the efficiency of communication. Remarkable progress in the fields of psychology and natural language processing (NLP) has paved the way for training AI systems to communicate ideas in diverse manners. Our research endeavors encompassed an investigation into the influence of physicians' personality traits on their medical practices and clinical performance (Ding, Lu, and Kannan 2022). Through the application of NLP methods, we successfully identified physicians' personality traits and validated these measures using clinical data. By incorporating users' personality traits into the AI algorithm, we can substantially enhance the efficiency and effectiveness of communication between physicians and AI. Consequently, AI-generated recommendations become more readily accepted by physicians, further reinforcing their trust in AI.

The third pivotal aspect crucial to instilling confidence in AI among physicians centers on accuracy. A noteworthy example that has garnered attention pertains to the emergence of ChatGPT, a question-answering bot developed by OpenAI, which has gained popularity. However, it encountered resistance within certain communities due to its proclivity for providing incorrect answers at a high frequency, leading to the temporary ban of ChatGPT on platforms like Stack Overflow (Vigliarolo 2022). While ChatGPT boasts the capability to engage in human-like conversations, one of the primary challenges faced by such communication bots lies in coding issues that contribute to inaccuracies in answering questions. It becomes evident that accuracy serves as the cornerstone for physicians to place their trust in AI systems. By prioritizing and ensuring the utmost accuracy in AI-generated recommendations, we can instill greater confidence in physicians and solidify their reliance on AI as a valuable tool in healthcare decision making.

Furthermore, alongside coding challenges, the effective management of data emerges as another critical factor influencing the accuracy of AI-generated recommendations. As underscored in the works of Dranove and Gaithwaite (2022) and Sahni et al. (2022), access to clean and dependable data assumes paramount importance when training AI systems. The presence of practice variations within healthcare settings can potentially impede the learning process of AI algorithms and hinder their ability to pass external validation.

In conclusion, the potential of clinical analytics to empower physicians with accurate diagnoses and appropriate treatment plans is significant, but it faces challenges akin to those encountered in insurers' utilization review processes. Overcoming these challenges requires addressing coding issues, effectively managing data, and accounting for practice variations, all of which contribute to reinforcing trust and acceptance of AI-generated recommendations among physicians. As Dranove and Garthwaite (2022) aptly stated, "This creates a tension: Is it better to force potentially biased physicians to conform to norms, or allow them to make their own decisions, factoring in idiosyncrasies? . . . AI does not eliminate this tension, but it may tilt the calculus."

Looking ahead, it is essential to prioritize research that addresses critical questions in the pursuit of establishing and strengthening physician trust in AI. Some of these pressing research questions include:

1. How can AI effectively deliver information to physicians? Understanding the mechanisms through which AI systems relay information to physicians is crucial for optimizing their acceptance and integration into clinical workflows. Investigating user-friendly interfaces, tailored communication

methods, and the appropriate timing of AI recommendations are areas that warrant further exploration.

2. What is the impact of incorporating AI recommendations on health outcomes? Evaluating the tangible impact of integrating AI-generated recommendations into clinical decision-making processes is paramount. Examining improvements in accuracy, timeliness, cost-effectiveness, and other aspects of patient outcomes can provide critical evidence to further validate the value of AI in healthcare.

3. Why do we need physicians if AI systems have the potential to make superior clinical decisions? Understanding the unique and irreplaceable role of physicians in the healthcare ecosystem, even in the presence of advanced AI systems, is vital. Uncovering the complementary nature of physician expertise, patient interaction, and ethical decision making alongside AI support is essential for building trust and establishing appropriate roles for both physicians and AI.

4. What incentives exist for physicians to develop trust in AI? Identifying the factors that motivate physicians to embrace and trust AI as a valuable tool is crucial. Exploring aspects such as improved clinical outcomes, enhanced efficiency, reduced workload, and opportunities for professional development can shed light on the motivational factors that drive physician acceptance and adoption of AI in their practice.

By addressing these research questions, we can gain valuable insights that guide the development of effective strategies and policies aimed at building and nurturing physician trust in AI. Ultimately, this will foster a harmonious collaboration between human expertise and technological advancements in healthcare.

References

Ding, J., S. F. Lu, and K. Kannan. 2022. "What Can Online Personal Statements Tell Us? Insights about Physicians' Personality Traits and Their Medical Performance." Working Paper, Purdue University.

Dranove, D., and C. Garthwaite. 2022. "Artificial Intelligence, the Evolution of the Healthcare Value Chain, and the Future of the Physician." This volume.

Sahni, N., G. Stein, R. Zemmel, and D. Cutler. 2022. "The Potential Impact of Artificial Intelligence on Healthcare Administrative Spending." This volume.

Vigliarolo, B. "Stack Overflow Bans ChatGPT as 'Substantially Harmful' for Coding Issues." *The Register*, December 5, 2022. https://www.theregister.com/2022/12/05/stack_overflow_bans_chatgpt/.

Comment on Chapters 1 and 2   Idris Adjerid

Insights from Adoption of Electronic Health Records

After two days of insightful research questions, rigorous evaluation of these questions, and thought-provoking discussion, it was a comment by David Chan at Stanford that stuck with me. He asked whether many of the questions we were asking about AI in healthcare were largely answered by the body of work evaluating how the diffusion of electronic health records (EHR) (the most recent large-scale digital push in healthcare) impacted different aspects of healthcare delivery.

The insights learned from the study of EHR diffusion and their impact on healthcare will almost certainly apply to the diffusion of AI in healthcare. Like EHR, effective use by clinicians, alignment of incentives, and reworking processes to incorporate insights from AI will be vital to realizing value. New scholarship considering these dynamics in the context of AI will certainly add value to the discourse and should be generally publishable. However, my conclusion from the day is that pathbreaking scholarships will need to think deeply about the unique aspects of AI and how these aspects will impact healthcare. A few examples come to mind of the kinds of questions future work could explore:

- Health economists have extensively studied competitive dynamics in healthcare. This body of work highlights, among other things, how regional healthcare monopolies contribute to reduced quality and efficiency (Gaynor 2007). How will AI impact these dynamics in ways that EHR did not? Will AI's potential to substitute for human capital in healthcare reduce barriers to entry and enable leaner entrants to disrupt healthcare at scale? Or, will data-rich incumbents leverage the AI revolution to further entrench themselves in these markets?
- EHR were largely focused on digitization of healthcare and provided, by and large, deterministic insights (e.g., identifying drug interactions for patients). How will the probabilistic nature of insights from AI impact use and adoption by clinicians? Will the encroachment of AI into domains that were core to physicians' value-add (e.g., diagnosis) impact these dynamics? Considering the potential of clinicians to reject certain types of AI insights, will be it optimal at times to reduce exposure to or scope of AI insights?
- Will integration of AI into healthcare shift patient demand, and in

Idris Adjerid is an associate professor in Business Information Technology at the Pamplin College of Business at Virginia Tech.

For acknowledgments, sources of research support, and disclosure of the author's material financial relationships, if any, please see https://www.nber.org/books-and-chapters/economics -artificial-intelligence-health-care-challenges/insights-adoption-ehr.

which directions? Under which conditions will lower-cost, more accessible, AI-powered services prosper and when will the human touch present in traditional healthcare prevail? The answer to these questions is not clear ex ante. In the context of mental health (a context where privacy and human interaction are key), AI-powered technology platforms for providing mental health services have been highly successful.[1]

Overall, the outlook for research at the intersection of AI and healthcare is bright, and there are several exciting areas for researchers to explore. I encourage myself and other researchers to be thoughtful about their pursuits in this space and look forward to research that helps healthcare integrate AI in ways that maximize welfare across the board.

Reference

Gaynor, M. 2007. "Competition and Quality in Health Care Markets." *Foundations and Trends® in Microeconomics* 2 (6): 441–508.

Comment on Chapters 1 and 3   M. Kate Bundorf
and Maria Polyakova

Artificial Intelligence and Decision Making in Health Care:
Prediction or Preferences?

People make most of their decisions in the context of uncertainty. Because each of our decisions can have many possible outcomes, we can never know with certainty how the choices we make today will affect us tomorrow. In the canonical economic model, people make decisions under uncertainty by assessing both the likelihood of potential outcomes associated with alternative courses of action and their utility of each outcome and then

M. Kate Bundorf is the J. Alexander McMahon Distinguished Professor of Health Policy and Management and a professor in the Sanford School of Public Policy and the Department of Population Health Sciences at Duke University, a core faculty member at the Duke-Margolis Center for Health Policy, and a research associate of the National Bureau of Economic Research.

Maria Polyakova is an assistant professor in the Department of Health Policy at Stanford University School of Medicine, and a faculty research fellow of the National Bureau of Economic Research.

For acknowledgments, sources of research support, and disclosure of the authors' material financial relationships, if any, please see https://www.nber.org/books-and-chapters/economics -artificial-intelligence-health-care-challenges/artificial-intelligence-and-decision-making -healthcare-prediction-or-preferences.

1. See https://www.brookings.edu/techstream/the-wellness-industrys-risky-embrace-of-ai -driven-mental-health-care/.

choosing the alternative with the greatest expected utility (Morgenstern and Von Neumann 1953; Savage 1954). In this model, people need two types of information to make a choice among alternatives: the distribution of future outcomes associated with each alternative, and how they value each of the possible future outcomes. Here we refer to the first as "prediction" and the second as "preferences." This distinction is consistent with the theoretical model developed by Agrawal, Gans, and Goldfarb (2018a), which differentiates between prediction and "judgment" in understanding the impact of artificial intelligence on decision making.

The distinction between prediction and preferences is central for understanding how artificial intelligence will impact health care treatment decisions. Uncertainty is at the heart of clinical decision making; both diagnosis and treatment are probabilistic. A well-working AI tool can be enormously beneficial for understanding the distribution of potential diagnoses and treatment outcomes. As Obermeyer and Mullainathan discuss in this volume, there are important challenges in generating predictions and deploying them in clinical settings including incomplete or biased data, challenges of communicating algorithmic predictions to human experts, and barriers to implementation. Overall, however, prediction is essential for clinical medicine and prediction technologies can reduce the cost or increase the quality of this important input into decision making (Agrawal et al. 2018b).

The ability of artificial intelligence to incorporate patient preference into decision making, however, is less straightforward. Clinical decision making requires interpreting information about probabilistic outcomes for patients. In many cases, this requires making trade-offs among uncertain, even if well-predicted outcomes. Patient preferences are critical for making these trade-offs. A challenge, which we explored empirically in the context of expert advice for the choice of health insurance plans (Bundorf, Polyakova, and Tai-Seale 2019), is that patients may not have full information about their own preferences. Analogously, in many clinical settings, patients may not have well-formed preferences over treatment outcomes. Indeed a key component of decision aids for health care treatment decisions is helping patients understand "either explicitly or implicitly, the value they place on potential benefits and harms" (Stacey et al. 2017). Physicians and other types of clinicians, due to their experience and expertise, naturally play a role in helping patients formulate their preferences. Can AI do this instead?

We propose that existing AI approaches to advising consumers based on their preferences are less well suited to health care decision making than in other contexts. A common data-driven approach for capturing preferences is to link the decisions of millions of consumers with objective measures of choice satisfaction to predict whether someone with your characteristics is likely to be satisfied with a particular option. This "consumers-like-you" approach, however, has limitations for decision making in health care. It assumes consumers are making good decisions, when we have lots of evidence that they aren't (Bernheim, DellaVigna, and Laibson 2019). Indeed, if consumers "like you" made great decisions, then they wouldn't need anyone's advice.

An alternative approach is to provide machine-based expert advice. This type of advice, however, imposes expert preferences on individual choices—in essence, assuming away preference heterogeneity across patients, the type of information we wanted to incorporate in the first place. Whether such computerized experts can replace today's physicians depends on how much we think physicians are able to tailor their expert advice to each patient. Physicians are under increasing pressure to provide that type of personalized advice due to a movement toward "shared decision making," in which patients are full partners with clinicians in health care decision making as opposed to more passive recipients of expert advice (Resnicow et al. 2022). The objective of shared decision making is to ensure that treatment decisions more fully reflect patient values. Patients may prefer tailored even if imperfect advice to a recommendation that is only right for an average patient.

As long as AI remains limited in its ability to "predict" patient preferences, it will remain a complement rather than a substitute for many physicians. As Dranove and Garthwaite in this volume recognize, medical specialties that focus less on patient relationships may be more substitutable by AI. Indeed, as AI tools become better at predicting the probabilities of different potential outcomes, the role of physicians is likely to shift more to the domain of helping patients formulate their preferences in response to AI-generated information.

To summarize, what are the implications of the distinction between prediction and preferences for the role of AI in health care decision making? AI's current state as a data prediction exercise may limit its ability to inform decisions that are highly dependent on preferences or decisions for which patient preferences vary substantially. Clinicians who help patients translate prediction into decisions by incorporating patient preferences will have skills that are complementary to the strengths of AI. Paradoxically, this implies that in contrast to the fear of AI replacing the medical profession promulgated by some, increased integration of AI into a clinician's daily routine may not replace physicians but rather incentivize physicians to focus on what medical students often say motivated them to choose medicine—listening to the patient.

References

Agrawal, Ajay, Joshua Gans, and Avi Goldfarb. 2018a. "Prediction, Judgment, and Complexity: A Theory of Decision-Making and Artificial Intelligence." In *The Economics of Artificial Intelligence: An Agenda*, edited by Ajay Agrawal, Joshua Gans, and Avi Goldfarb, 89–110. Chicago: University of Chicago Press.

Agrawal, Ajay, Joshua Gans, and Avi Goldfarb. 2018b. *Prediction Machines: The Simple Economics of Artificial Intelligence*. Boston: Harvard Business Press.

Bernheim, B. Douglas, Stefano DellaVigna, and David Laibson. 2019. *Handbook of Behavioral Economics-Foundations and Applications 2*. Amsterdam: North-Holland.

Bundorf, M. Kate, Maria Polyakova, and Ming Tai-Seale. 2019. "How Do Humans Interact with Algorithms? Experimental Evidence from Health Insurance." NBER Working Paper No. 25976. Cambridge, MA: National Bureau of Economic Research.

Morgenstern, Oskar, and John Von Neumann. 1953. *Theory of Games and Economic Behavior*. Princeton, NJ: Princeton University Press.

Resnicow, Ken, Delwyn Catley, Kathy Goggin, Sarah Hawley, and Geoffrey C. Williams. 2022. "Shared Decision Making in Health Care: Theoretical Perspectives for Why It Works and for Whom." *Medical Decision Making* 42 (6): 755–64.

Savage, Leonard J. 1954. *The Foundations of Statistics*. New York: John Wiley & Sons.

Stacey, Dawn, France Légaré, Krystina Lewis, Michael J. Barry, Carol L. Bennett, Karen B. Eden, Margaret Holmes-Rovner, Hilary Llewellyn-Thomas, Anne Lyddiatt, Richard Thomson, and Lyndal Trevena. 2017. "Decision Aids for People Facing Health Treatment or Screening Decisions." *Cochrane Database of Systematic Reviews* 4 (4): CD001431.

Comment on Chapters 1 and 4   W. Nicholson Price II

Health AI, System Performance, and Physicians in the Loop

Accounts of artificial intelligence (AI) in medicine must grapple, in one way or another, with the interaction between AI systems and the humans involved in delivering healthcare. Humans are, of course, involved throughout the process of developing, deploying, and evaluating AI systems, but a particular role stands out: the human in the loop of an algorithmic decision. In medicine, when an algorithm is involved in a decision, a typical view of the system envisions a human healthcare professional mediating that algorithm—deciding whether and how to implement or react to any recommendation, prediction, or other algorithmic output. This person is the human in the loop, and their role is often central, complicated, and contested.

Principal contributions to this volume recognize the key role of humans in the loop. Dranove and Garthwaite (2023) focus on the value chain of healthcare and the physician's role within it, recapitulating the notion of the

W. Nicholson Price II is a professor at University of Michigan Law School and a senior fellow at the University of Copenhagen Centre for Advanced Studies in Biomedical Innovation Law.

For acknowledgments, sources of research support, and disclosure of the author's material financial relationships, if any, please see https://www.nber.org/books-and-chapters/economics-artificial-intelligence-health-care-challenges/health-ai-system-performance-and-physicians-loop.

physician as captain of the ship—a key human-in-the-loop conception—and recognizing that AI's contribution, and who will capture its value in the healthcare delivery setting, depends in some part on its role in substituting for that human role versus complementing it. Lakkarju and Farronato (2022), in ongoing work presented at the conference but not included in this volume, elucidate the complexities of physician–algorithm interactions in terms of system performance. They demonstrate that when physicians using AI systems are provided with explanations of the system's recommendations, their performance may be better or worse than the system alone, depending on how accurate and complete those explanations are. Physicians provided with small amounts of accurate information about the model's recommendations performed worse than the model alone; those who received substantial accurate information did better, but those who received substantial information that was somewhat accurate did worse. The effects are complex and nonintuitive. And even the regulatory regime described by Stern (2023) turns on the role of the human in the loop, whether that human is the intended user of an FDA-regulated system (and thus intended but not required to use the system as labeled) or the adequately informed human user of clinical decision support software (and thus rendering the system outside FDA's regulatory authority) (US FDA 2022).

Conceptions of AI systems in health typically envision the human in the loop as a well-trained, well-resourced physician with adequate resources and adequate time. But variations in who the human in the loop is, what they can do, the context in which they do it, and what they are supposed to be doing in the first place may substantially change how the whole system functions and the economic implications of that function. Consider two perturbations: what the human in the loop is supposed to be doing, and the capabilities of the human who occupies that role.

First, system designers, patients, health systems, and physicians may have very different visions of what the human in the loop is supposed to be doing, whether implicitly or explicitly, and these visions may be in substantial tension (Crootof, Kaminski, and Price 2023). The most obvious role for a physician in the loop of an algorithmic system is to increase accuracy—indeed, this conception underlies Lakkarju and Farronato's evaluation of the success of different AI explanatory models (2023). But a conception of physicians as only improving the system's *overall* performance may align poorly with the expectations of patients, who would likely prefer that physicians prioritize their own individual outcomes, regardless of that prioritization's impact on overall systemic accuracy or efficiency. Or patients and patient advocates may prefer that physicians not defer to AI systems because they consider machine decision making to be deleterious to patient dignity, and want a human role in protecting that dignity (Crootof Kaminski, and Price 2023). On the other hand, whatever the impact on efficiency or accuracy, physicians themselves may prefer to remain in control—and avoid deference—because the role of physician as the knowledgeable captain of the healthcare ship is essential to physician job security and prestige. These implicit or explicit roles may easily conflict, and unless system designers and regulators construct the physician–system interactions quite carefully, those conflicts can easily go unnoticed and unresolved.

Second, even assuming alignment of roles and incentives (and here let us assume a role focused on purely on accuracy), the human who is actually in the loop of an algorithmic system may be substantially different from the human assumed by system designers, users, or regulators. In particular, expectations may often be significantly higher than reality. Not all healthcare providers will be able, adequately trained, or well resourced enough to catch errors in the system or to ensure that it works as intended, especially in settings that differ significantly from those in which the algorithm was developed (Price 2020).

Consider regulators. In October 2022, FDA issued a final guidance laying out how it evaluates whether software is clinical decision support software (US FDA 2022). Such software, which is intended merely to inform physicians and to give them adequate information to evaluate the software's recommendations, has been congressionally defined as not a medical device and therefore outside FDA's regulatory authority (21 U.S.C. § 360j[o][1][E]). And so FDA carefully considered what software needs to do to fall within this exception: It cannot be time-critical, because humans would tend to rely on the software in a crunch; it cannot provide only one recommendation, because humans would tend to defer; and it must provide a large amount of information to support its recommendations, because humans need that information to evaluate that recommendation (US FDA 2022). In this vision, an adequately enabled human in the loop ensures that the system will not dominate the care decision process, which therefore removes the need for a heavy regulatory hand. But of course, all this relies on a healthcare professional who has the time, training, and inclination to evaluate and review recommendations even when the decision is *not* time-critical, rather than just picking the top off the list of ranked recommendations and going along with that recommendation. That vision of a healthcare professional in the loop may not accurately reflect the human filling the role; healthcare professionals are always pressed for time and already burned out on computer-related tasks (Downing, Bates, and Longhurst 2018).

Overly prescriptive or demanding assumptions about humans in the loop are likely to result in systemic underperformance. If system designers, implementers, and regulators assume a time-rich expert and bake that assumption into AI design, the absence of that expert could easily cause system failure—though whether that failure is obvious, catastrophic, or insidiously opaque will depend on the particulars of the system and its failure mode (Choi 2019). But an expert human in the loop need not be assumed. Sometimes, indeed, AI systems may need to be designed to be almost totally agnostic as to who is the human in the loop, what role they might perform, and what training or resources they may have available.

Taking it one step further, the value of AI systems in healthcare settings may in fact be greatest in situations where human experts are *least* available. A key potential role of AI systems is to democratize expertise and to make formerly specialist capabilities available more widely (Price 2019). Some systems do this explicitly—the IDx-DR diabetic retinopathy diagnosis system aims to provide broad access to a diagnostic tool formerly only available with the assistance of an ophthalmologist, and other systems in development aim for similar breadth (Grzybowski et al., 2019). Other systems may achieve such broad reach only by use far beyond their FDA-cleared label or other intended use. But they may nonetheless bring healthcare capacity to many otherwise underserved individuals, whether domestically or internationally, and this result should be celebrated even if it is harder to evaluate or reimburse.

Humans in the loop are key to considerations of AI systems in health as in other fields. What those humans are supposed to do, the resources they have available, and even who stands in the room in the first place all underlie how well the system works and who ultimately benefits.

References

Choi, Bryan. 2019. "Crashworthy Code." *Washington Law Review* 94: 39–117.

Crootof, Rebecca, Margot E. Kaminski, and W. Nicholson Price II. 2023. "Humans in the Loop." *Vanderbilt Law Review* 76 (2): 429–510.

Downing, N. Lance, David W. Bates, and Christopher A. Longhurst. 2018. "Physician Burnout in the Electronic Health Record Era: Are We Ignoring the Real Cause?" *Annals of Internal Medicine* 169 (1): 50–52.

Dranove, David, and Craig Garthwaite. 2023. "Artificial Intelligence, the Evolution of the Healthcare Value Chain, and the Future of the Physician." This volume.

Grzybowski, Andrzej, Piotr Brona, Gilbert Lim, Paisan Ruamviboonsuk, Gavin S. W. Tan, Michael Abramoff, and Daniel S. W. Ting. 2020. "Artificial Intelligence for Diabetic Retinopathy Screening: A Review." *Eye* 34: 451–60.

Lakkarju, Himabindu, and Chiara Farronato. 2022. "When Algorithms Explain Themselves: AI Adoption and Accuracy of Experts' Decisions." Presented at NBER Conference on Economics of Artificial Intelligence, Toronto, September 22–23, 2022.

Price, W. Nicholson, II. 2019. "Artificial Intelligence in the Medical System: Four Roles for Potential Transformation." *Yale Journal of Health Policy, Law, and Ethics* 18 (3): 122–32.

Price, W. Nicholson, II. 2020. "Medical AI and Contextual Bias." *Harvard Journal of Law & Technology* 33 (1): 66–116.

Stern, Ariel Dora. 2023. "The Regulation of Medical AI: Policy Approaches, Data, and Innovation Incentives." This volume.

US FDA (Food and Drug Administration). 2022. "Clinical Decision Support Software: Guidance for Industry and Food and Drug Administration Staff." https://www.fda.gov/regulatory-information/search-fda-guidance-documents/clinical-decision-support-software.

Comment on Chapters 1–4   Laura C. Rosella

Building Blocks for AI in Health Care

Advances in AI are increasing rapidly across many sectors; however, the impact in health care has been more limited in comparison. It has become clear that health care's complexity, system actors, data context, and regulatory requirements necessitate a different approach. This comment will discuss themes relating to health decision making, data challenges, and the potential for regulatory innovation raised by the contributing authors to this volume.

Across the invited papers, the complexity of the health care environment and, more specifically, the motivations, actors, and built-in incentives were articulated. Together these factors drive the unique context in which health care operates and point to advances needed for the next phase of health AI. In health care, where decisions have significant implications for patient care, there is an understandable reluctance to rely on AI, despite several examples highlighted across the papers that show improved accuracy and economic benefits. Health care decisions vary widely across clinical tasks and inherently involve trust at multiple levels. There is obvious trust needed between the patient and health care provider; however, there is an equally important level of trust required by clinicians and the measured or observed information about their patients that is the basis of their clinical decisions. In health care, there has been an increasing trend toward transparency and explicit reasoning over the past four decades, particularly following the evidence-based medicine movement (Scott, Cook, and Coiera 2021). For AI to translate from a well-developed idea to day-to-day impact, designing for this decision-making context is needed. (Bottou 2014) The future of AI in health care will require intentional and specific design that allows for transparency, trust, and justification of decisions. To inform this evolution, there is a need for real-world testing with rigorous evaluations within health care environments. These evaluations will inform how to optimize AI that overcomes the identified barriers related to decision making.

Increasing trust in AI can be enhanced by providing information alongside AI to support reasoning, but equally important is to ensure trusted systems are in place for oversight and monitoring. One of the main concerns about the uptake of AI in health care is the potential harm due to systematic prediction errors, especially for those that already face discrimination in society (Obermeyer et al. 2019). Ultimately, in order to instill confidence

Laura C. Rosella is an associate professor in the Dalla Lana School of Public Health at the University of Toronto, where she holds Canada Research Chair in Population Health Analytics.

For acknowledgments, sources of research support, and disclosure of the author's material financial relationships, if any, please see https://www.nber.org/books-and-chapters/economics -artificial-intelligence-health-care-challenges/building-blocks-ai-healthcare.

for use in health care environments, there is a need to ensure transparency, reproducibility, and rigor in the validation of models that underpin AI (Rosella 2022). To ensure this oversight takes place independently, systematically, and appropriately for AI, it needs to be backed by the regulatory innovations called for in Stern's analysis.

The implementation of electronic medical records (EMRs) in health care has resulted in numerous challenges and unintended consequences, including provider burnout (Li et al. 2022). Those who work in health care frequently argue that EMRs were not set up to succeed in the realities of health care and should serve as an important lesson to those developing AI technologies. To avoid a similar fate, there should be an initial phase of intense study of the health care setting, for example, through ethnographic approaches. By contrast, most AI developed for health care start with the data generated from health care and build the technology from there. One needed change would be to instead start with the people and environments before the data and algorithms. By designing for the health care context first, there is an increased likelihood of adoption and opportunities to build trust and accountability, thereby forming the basis for change and improvement.

All papers in this volume reflect on the challenges with health data quality and the barriers to data access. Increased granularity of health data, more comprehensive data elements, and open data access are essential to build, validate, and update AI models, but the challenge of health data access proves to be one of health care's most thorny problems. Several new data platform models are now emerging, aiming to balance the ethical and confidential use of personal health information with the need for transparency, reproducibility, and diversity of data required for robust AI. Obermeyer presents a proposed data platform solution representing a welcome shift in the health data ecosystem. Ongoing work linking multiple data streams, including capturing people's sociodemographic and environmental characteristics, will be needed to improve AI performance and mitigate against potential biases.

The papers in this volume point to the building blocks needed for AI to have a meaningful impact in health care. The first is acknowledging and designing AI to support the reasoning and transparency needed for health care decisions. Second is the need for an intentional and more detailed understanding of the complex health care environment, behaviors, and motivations within in order to design AI solutions that work with and not against these realities. Third, efforts must be made to enrich the data used to develop AI, and there is a continued need to ensure this data is made available in a responsible way that allows for improved AI performance, fairness, and reproducibility. Finally, there is a clear need for innovative models of regulation and continuous oversight of AI used in health care that measures performance over time and the impact on patient outcomes.

References

Bottou, L. 2014. "From Machine Learning to Machine Reasoning." *Machine Learning* 94 (2): 133–49. https://doi.org/10.1007/s10994-013-5335-x.

Li, C., C. Parpia, A. Sriharan, and D. T. Keefe. 2022. "Electronic Medical Record-Related Burnout in Healthcare Providers: A Scoping Review of Outcomes and Interventions." *BMJ Open* 12 (8): e060865. https://doi.org/10.1136/bmjopen-2022-060865.

Obermeyer, Z., B. Powers, C. Vogeli, and S. Mullainathan. 2019. "Dissecting Racial Bias in an Algorithm Used to Manage the Health of Populations." *Science* 366 (6464): 447–53. https://doi.org/10.1126/science.aax2342.

Rosella, L. C. 2022. "Deep Learning Approaches Applied to Routinely Collected Health Data: Future Directions." *International Journal of Epidemiology* 51 (3): 931–33. https://doi.org/10.1093/ije/dyac064.

Scott, I., D. Cook, and E. Coiera. 2021. "Evidence-Based Medicine and Machine Learning: A Partnership with a Common Purpose." *BMJ Evidence-Based Medicine* 26 (6): 290–94. https://doi.org/10.1136/bmjebm-2020-111379.

Author Index

Subject Index